STUDIES IN
HIGHER EDUCATION

Edited by
Philip G. Altbach
Lynch School of Education, Boston College

A ROUTLEDGE SERIES

Studies in Higher Education

Philip G. Altbach, *General Editor*

WHEN FOR-PROFIT MEETS NONPROFIT
EDUCATING THROUGH THE MARKET

Jared L. Bleak

Routledge
New York & London

Published in 2005 by
Routledge
Taylor & Francis Group
270 Madison Ave,
New York NY 10016

Published in Great Britain by
Routledge
Taylor & Francis Group
2 Park Square,
Milton Park, Abingdon,
Oxon, OX14 4RN

Transferred to Digital Printing 2010

International Standard Book Number-10: 0-415-97417-8 (Hardcover)
International Standard Book Number-13: 978-0-415-97417-2 (Hardcover)
Library of Congress Card Number 2004029663

Library of Congress Cataloging-In-Publication Data

Bleak, Jared L.
    When for-profit meets nonprofit : educating through the market / Jared L. Bleak.
        p. cm. -- (RoutledgeFalmer studies in higher education)
    Includes bibliographical references.
    ISBN 0-415-97417-8 (hardback)
    1. Education, Higher--Economic aspects--United States. 2. Business and education--United States. I. Title. II. Series: RoutledgeFalmer studies in higher education (Unnumbered)

LC67.62.B54 2005
338.4'3378--dc22
2004029663

ISBN10: 0-415-97417-8 (hbk)
ISBN10: 0-415-88246-X (pbk)

ISBN13: 978-0-415-97417-2 (hbk)
ISBN13: 978-0-415-88246-0 (pbk)

Taylor & Francis Group
is the Academic Division of T&F Informa plc.

Visit the Taylor & Francis Web site at
http://www.taylorandfrancis.com

and the Routledge Web site at
http://www.routledge-ny.com

For Julie, with love and gratitude

Contents

Acknowledgments

Nothing significant is ever achieved alone. I am indebted to many individuals for their help and support.

I thank first and foremost, my advisor and doctoral committee chair, Dick Chait. He has not only guided me in the process from first draft to final copy, but contributed throughout by pushing my thinking and sharpening my ideas. Mercifully, his high standards and expectations were always leavened with words of encouragement and confidence. He is an amazing person and has been a trusted mentor, advocate, and critic. His guidance has made my Harvard experience what I had hoped it would be.

Judy McLaughlin, doctoral committee member, has such a thoughtful and compassionate way of interacting with students. I have appreciated her many kindnesses since my first days on campus as a master's student. I am also grateful for her sharp eye and keen insight, which have made this book much better than it would otherwise have been.

Jim Honan, doctoral committee member, has exemplified to me the qualities of a superb teacher, a skilled administrator, and a trusted colleague. His confidence in my own teaching, writing, and research abilities was a boon throughout my studies. His support through this process has meant a great deal.

This book would not have been possible without the generous help and time of faculty, administrators, and trustees of Columbia, Duke, NYU, and Babson, as well as the managers of Fathom, Duke CE, NYUonline, and Babson Interactive. I am grateful to the many who willingly gave of their time and expertise in interviews and in subsequent conversations.

I am also indebted to Cathy Trower for her support and continual expressions of confidence. She has taught me a great deal and has been a trusted mentor. I am especially grateful for the jump-start she gave me by reading a preliminary draft of the book's first two chapters. She provided just what I needed to get through my "writer's block" and move forward.

Many friends and peers have provided immeasurable help. Frances Shavers has been a good friend throughout graduate school. Susan Kardos and Michal Kurlaender provided excellent advice and helpful motivation as study group members. Heidi Neiman, Matt Hartley, Sue Stuebner, and Heather Peske have provided timely words of encouragement.

The Governance Futures Project has provided a wonderful learning laboratory for me to participate with Bill Ryan, Barbara Taylor, and Dick in designing the future of nonprofit governance. Rather than treating me as a student, they have regarded me as a peer and colleague. I have appreciated their trust and confidence. Members of the Harvard Project on Faculty Appointments—Bill Mallon, Cheryl Sternman Rule, Kerryann O'Meara, Laura Couturier, Jordan Bach—offered encouragement and support.

My children have been faithful cheerleaders throughout. No child's prayer was uttered without a plea for "Daddy's dissertation." My own and Julie's parents have been ever ready with words of encouragement and faith.

Most of all, I owe everything to Julie, my wife and best friend. She has endured the highs and lows of this experience and never wavered. Her unfailing love has made all the difference.

Preface

This book addresses the increasing tumult over the commercialization of higher education—a battle over profit and principle, money and mission. While many issues in higher education encompass the mission and values of the university, the operation of for-profit subsidiaries by nonprofit universities provides the potential for an especially contentious clash.

In this book, I explain why four highly regarded nonprofit universities established for-profit subsidiaries to market and distribute online education, despite a culture clash in some cases, and detail how these companies were governed in relation to their nonprofit parents. In this effort, I have endeavored to write a "vivid portrait," rather than a "wearisome report" (Chaffee & Tierney, 1988, p. 15), by weaving the literature together with the experiences of each of these companies. I have used organizational culture theory as the guiding conceptual framework and analytical lens in this research. Though the research was conducted according to qualitative case-based methodology, nowhere do I present a complete case. Instead, I discuss findings by theme and topic in each chapter.

SIGNIFICANCE FOR RESEARCH AND PRACTICE

This book aims to contribute to the understanding of the governance and culture of higher education. This analysis will interest university presidents and boards of trustees who are considering the creation of a for-profit subsidiary or are currently governing one, faculty members at these institutions, and scholars and observers of the academy.

Studying governance through the lens of organizational culture has many benefits. Since culture concerns "decisions, actions, and communication" (Tierney, 1991, p. 127), leaders in higher education need to understand their organization's culture. In addition, higher education institutions lack explicit and implicit control mechanisms (Cohen & March, 1974; March & Olsen, 1976; Masland, 1991). In that vacuum, organizational culture acts as an "unobtrusive organizational control" (Masland, 1991, p. 124), regulating behavior and actions (Schein, 1992).

Too often it seems institutional participants become aware of organizational culture only when its tenets are breached. Tierney (1991) commented:

> Only when we break these codes and conventions are we forcibly reminded of their presence and considerable power. Likewise, administrators tend to recognize their organization's culture only when they have transgressed its bounds and severe conflicts or adverse relationships ensue. As a result, we frequently find ourselves dealing with organizational culture in an atmosphere of crisis management, instead of reasoned reflection and consensual change. (p. 127)

As higher education moves from an "integrated academic culture" to "the many cultures of the conglomerate" (Clark, 1980, p. 25)—underscored by the creation of for-profit subsidiaries—a richer understanding of organizational culture will help "reduce adversarial relationships," "minimize the occurrence and consequences of cultural conflict," and "help foster the development of shared goals" (Tierney, 1991, p. 128). But more significantly, this book contributes to a better understanding of the larger controversy over whether universities have become too business-like, too market oriented, and whether they have sold their souls and values in the process. In essence, this study provides a window into whether it is possible to do business like a business—a trend afoot in the academy—and still retain allegiance to core values.

DEFINITIONS

In a legal sense, no one owns a nonprofit corporation (Goldstein, 2000b). In a for-profit corporation, however, investors receive ownership rights in exchange for a capital investment (e.g., money, equipment, property). These rights then entitle the owner to a share of earnings resulting from the corporation's activities. Upon dissolution of the company, any remaining assets are distributed to owners. A nonprofit organization, however, operates under the "nondistribution constraint" (Simon, 1987, p. 68), which forbids the distribution of profits or earnings to owners or investors (see also Goldstein, 2000b). Because it has no owners, a nonprofit corporation cannot issue shares or dividends to individuals, and upon dissolution, under Section 501(c)(3) of the Federal Tax Code, it must distribute its remaining assets to another nonprofit group with a similar mission or purpose (Silk, 1994).

As nonprofit organizations have become more market oriented, the establishment of for-profit subsidiaries has grown steadily (Simon, 1987). In determining whether or not a company is a subsidiary, ownership and control are the key criteria. According to section 368 of the Internal Revenue Code, a company is considered "a subsidiary if the parent owns 50 percent or more of the combined voting power of all classes of stock entitled to vote, or 50 percent or more of the total value of shares of all classes of stock outstanding" (IRC, 2002).

The relationship between a nonprofit organization (or a for-profit corporation) and its subsidiaries is commonly described as "parent/subsidiary." In this relationship, though the parent is responsible for incorporating the subsidiary, naming its board and officers, and establishing its purpose, the subsidiary is nonetheless recognized by the parent and by outside parties as an independent corporation, managed by its own board of directors as it pursues its purpose (Thompson, 2003).

A NOTE ON METHODOLOGY

This study used qualitative case study methodology to analyze the governance of four for-profit subsidiaries. The four subsidiaries—Babson Interactive, Duke Corporate Education, Fathom, and NYUonline—along with each company's parent institution, Babson College, Duke University, Columbia University, and New York University, respectively, were chosen through a criteria-sampling strategy (Miles & Huberman, 1994), based on the following criteria: (1) the for-profit subsidiary was established by a non-profit college or university; (2) the for-profit subsidiary had an established organizational structure and was in operation for at least six months; (3) the president of the university and the CEO of the subsidiary and most key leaders of both organizations were accessible to interview and have granted their permission. In addition, I restricted the study to private colleges and universities because of significant and intrinsic differences in the governance of public and private institutions.

The four parent institutions selected for the study provide four distinct vantage points from which to view the governance and culture of their subsidiaries. Three of the institutions—Duke, Columbia, and NYU—are classified as *doctoral/research universities—extensive* according to the Carnegie system, while Babson College is classified as a *school of business and management*. NYU and Columbia are located in Manhattan, while Babson and Duke inhabit suburban campuses in Wellesley, Massachusetts, and Durham, North Carolina, respectively. They vary greatly by size, from 52,000 students at NYU to 3,431 at Babson.

Table 1-1. Comparison of Four Research Sites.

Institution	Location	Carnegie Classification	Total Enrollment (Fall 2002)	For-Profit Subsidiary	Founding of Subsidiary	Control
New York University	Manhattan, New York	Doctoral/Research Universities—Extensive	51,9011[1]	NYUonline Inc.	1998 (closed January 2002)	Private
Columbia University	Manhattan, New York	Doctoral/Research Universities—Extensive	20,028[2]	Fathom, Inc.	2000 (closed January 2003)	Private
Duke University	Durham, North Carolina	Doctoral/Research Universities—Extensive	11,504[3]	Duke Corporate Education Inc.	2000	Private
Babson College	Wellesley, Massachusetts	Schools of Business and Management	3,431[4]	Babson Interative, LLC	2000	Private

[1] Headcount enrollment; (14,751 of the 51,951 students enrolled are in non-credit programs); http://www.nyu.edu/search.nyu

[2] FTE enrollment; http://www.columbia.edu/cu/opir/2003EnrlPTFT.htm

[3] FTE enrollment; http://www.finsvc.duke.edu/finsvc/Resources/reports/financial_reports02.pdf

[4] FTE enrollment; http://www2.babson.edu/babson/BabsonHPp.nsf/Public/aboutBabsonglance#Student

Duke Corporate Education was created from Duke's Fuqua School of Business, a top-tier business school, while NYUonline and Fathom were established by the central administration and board of trustees of each subsidiary's parent institution, with no particular college or school affiliation. Additionally, Fathom was organized as a consortium of leading nonprofit educational and cultural organizations, with Columbia as the lead institution. Babson Interactive was founded essentially as an entrepreneurial endeavor of Babson College, whose institutional raison d'etre is entrepreneurship.

Data were collected through in-depth interviews and content analysis of internal and external documents. I interviewed key participants in the governance of both the university and the subsidiary, including those who were involved in the decision to create the for-profit subsidiary, those who were centrally involved in the company's operation and governance, and where available, the most influential critics of the new organization. In all, I conducted 49 interviews across the four research sites. Most of these interviews were accomplished during multiple-day site visits to each organization. Unless otherwise referenced, all quotes are from these personal interviews. Institutional documents, such as board meeting minutes, administrative memoranda, presentation material, and organizational policies, along with campus and national newspaper articles, and other external documents, were used to triangulate the interview data and corroborate accounts.

Appendix A provides a comprehensive account of the study's design and methodology.

ORGANIZATION

Chapter 1 introduces the controversy surrounding the escalating commercialization of higher education, one that centers on the discord between the values and basic assumptions that hold sway in the corporation and the academy. Chapter 2 discusses the rationale for the creation of the four subsidiaries in the study. The next four chapters discuss the key arenas where the two value systems generated the most heat and friction: governance, personnel, curriculum, and the role of the faculty. The book concludes with findings and implications for faculty and academic administrators.

Chapter One

Going to the Market

The pursuit of market-oriented activities by colleges and universities in search of new revenue streams, increased enrollments, greater prestige, and amplified visibility for their "brand names" became common practice in the late 1990's and the early 21st century. Marketing and promotional campaigns to increase revenues are now commonplace. Recently, fourteen public universities contracted with the Collegiate Licensing Corporation and the Starter athletic apparel company to display their logos on a Nascar series racecar, guaranteeing each institution royalty income from sales of related Nascar promotional items, an up-front payment for participating, and the opportunity to have their logo paraded before up to 90,000 fans on race day (Frye, 2001). Some universities sell to the highest bidder the naming rights to their sports arenas—e.g., Comcast Center at the University of Maryland and Save Mart Center at California State University at Fresno—while others have even joined the cola wars by signing lucrative contracts which guarantee soft drink companies exclusive "pouring rights" on their campuses (Suggs, 2000, January 14; Van Der Werf, 1999, October 15).

Commercialization may be most dramatic in athletics, with multimillion-dollar coaching contracts, ever-lengthening seasons, and game schedules created to accommodate television, regardless of students' academic schedules. Case in point—for two straight seasons the University of Oregon has rented space on a Manhattan skyscraper hoping to put its football program "on the national map" (Rhoden, 2002, July 25, p. D1). Said one university official, "If you're not located in a media center, you go to the center" (p. D1). In 2001, Oregon spent $250,000 on a banner near Madison Square Garden and in 2002, the price tag rose to $300,000 for a huge banner overlooking Times Square, beckoning passersby to ogle the university's star player and urging them to watch the team on television (Wojnarowski, 2002, August 9).

Following the example of the airlines, health clubs, and other industries that manage load factors and demand, the University of Oregon offered students discounts on afternoon courses, hoping to relieve some of the strain on resources during the more popular morning hours (Farrell, 2002, July 19). And, in an effort to keep students' disposable income on campus and create an additional source of revenue, many universities have purchased nearby hotels. Not surprisingly, these market-oriented activities have not been universally admired. Said one skeptic, "A university's core mission is not operating a hotel" (June, 2002, August 16, p. A29).

Similarly, these activities have been seen as reflecting a subtle change in how students are viewed: "Students are no longer seen as scholars, . . . but as profit centers" (Slaughter, 2001, p. 24). In the face of increasing competition to enroll and retain students, universities now build lavish dorm rooms with maid service, gargantuan fitness centers, and "food-courts" with gourmet menus. Driving the growth of amenities is the power students and parents have that comes with increased competition. Students act as consumers. One administrator frankly admitted, "The students say, 'What can you offer me?' So everybody's building new facilities to keep up with the Joneses" (Leonard, 2002, September 3, p. A1).

PROFITING FROM RESEARCH

The university economic engine ranks at the top of most state's goals for higher education. Nearly a third of the nation's governors have pressed their legislatures to increase funding for research and technology-transfer programs in public universities. Other states have eased restrictions on access to research facilities by for-profit companies (Schmidt, 2002, March 29). A leading example of the push for closer connection to business, North Carolina State University recently spent more than $250 million to create a 1,000-acre research park—Centennial Campus. Heralded by university officials as the "wave of the future of higher education," this "marriage of private industry and academe" (Carlson, 2000a, p. A49), houses scores of fledgling companies alongside academic departments and will feature a golf course, a light-rail system, housing, and a public middle school.

About 25 percent of the country's current non-profit business incubators (organizations formed to support the formation and growth of businesses), like those at North Carolina State, are run by universities and colleges, a trend likely to grow substantially (Carlson, 2000a; Van Der Werf & Blumenstyk, 2001). These incubators are now part of a considerable push by universities to profit from research.

"State lawmakers are no longer willing to support universities' research simply for the sake of expanding knowledge and improving the reputations of higher education institutions" (Schmidt, 2002, March 29). Politicians' pursuit of a return on the public's investment in higher education—in the form of revenues generated for products developed in university labs and through the creation and growth of companies developed with university technological innovations—has driven connections to industry. These companies mean jobs, increased tax revenues, and, as every politician hopes, votes (Lynton, 1989, Sept-Oct).

These actions highlight an apparent shift in how state legislatures and governors conceive of the role and purposes of universities. No longer viewed principally as a repository and cultivator of civic values, the public university is now seen primarily as a revenue generator and economic engine (Giroux & Myrsiades, 2001; Powers, Powers, Betz, & Aslanian, 1988).

At the federal level, market-oriented activities have been nurtured by legislation aimed specifically at increasing the contributions of universities to the national economy. The Bayh-Dole Act, passed by Congress in 1980, which allowed higher education institutions to patent the results of federally sponsored research, has served to "revolutionize university—industry relations" (Press and Washburn, 2000, March, p. 41). Since Bayh-Dole, the number of patent applications by universities has soared from an average of 250 per year in 1980, to 8,534 in 2000. Universities realized more than $1 billion in patent royalties in fiscal year 2000 alone (Blumenstyk, 2002, March 22), up from $641 million in 1999 (Blumenstyk, 2000). Fourteen institutions reported earnings on royalties in excess of $20 million in 2000, compared to only eight in 1999. The University of California system realized over $260 million in combined licensing income, while Columbia University alone earned over $138 million in 2000 (Blumenstyk, 2002, March 22). These examples underscore the comments of one observer, "Universities, once wary beneficiaries of corporate largesse, have become eager co-capitalists, embracing market values as never before" (Press & Washburn, 2000, March, p. 41).

Other connections between faculty research and corporations have been decried. The deal between Novartis, a pharmaceutical company, and the University of California at Berkeley was cited as prima facie evidence of the dangerous influence of corporations on the academy (Press & Washburn, 2000, March). Under the deal, Novartis agreed to fund $25 million in departmental research in exchange for first rights to negotiate licenses on discoveries as well as first look at all research produced by faculty members in the funded departments (including that paid for by state and federal agencies and private parties). To allow time to acquire patents on new technology, Novartis could ask for a publication to be delayed for up to 90 days (Blumenstyk, 2001, June 22). Arrangements such as these add to the "queasy suspicion that the process of discovery is in some way corrupted if it is driven by profit" (Economist, 2001, February 17, p. 21).

This suspicion prompted twelve medical journals to adopt a policy to assure the independence of industry-funded research, by rejecting manuscripts submitted by researchers "who did not have control of either the data or the decision on whether to publish results" (Guterman & Werf, 2001, October 5, p. A29)[1]. This action stemmed from several incidents where companies tried to silence economically disadvantageous research results. For example, a pharmaceutical company demanded up to $10 million from a researcher and his university as a result of research, published in *The Journal of the American Medical Association,* which concluded the company's drugs were not effective against the HIV virus (Mangan, 2000)[2]. Fears abound that many industry-sponsored research studies are biased in favor of the funders. A study in the *New England Journal of Medicine* that looked at 70 reviews of a heart drug substantiated this concern; the outcome of the review could be easily predicted by the reviewer's relationship to the manufacturer. "Ninety-six percent of those who found the drug safe had ties; among those with no commercial connection, only 63 percent concluded it was safe" (Ahuja, 2001, May 7).

FOR-PROFIT HIGHER EDUCATION

By creating innovative arrangements, non-profit colleges and universities are delivering curricula through for-profit subsidiaries aimed principally at the $3.5 billion online education market—a sector projected to expand to $7 billion nationally and $25 billion worldwide by 2003 (Eklund, 2001, January 26; Goldman, 2000; Rewick, 2001, March 12). The financial commitment to create a for-profit distance education subsidiary is substantial— NYUonline nearly $25 million and Columbia's Fathom upwards of $30 million. The intent of these investments, for some institutions, was to spawn subsidiaries that were considered more nimble, entrepreneurial, and adaptable than their comparatively staid non-profit parents (Goldstein, 2000b; Kwartler, 2000). Not surprisingly, these companies are built like businesses, where speed in decision-making and a strategic market orientation—qualities foreign to the traditional academy—are considered the *sine qua non* for success (Abel, 2000b; Davis & Botkin, 1994).

The impetus behind the creation of these subsidiaries has to some extent been the phenomenal growth of the for-profit higher education sector

(Goldstein, 2000b; Ruch, 2001). The number of for-profit, 4-year degree-granting institutions grew over 266 percent between 1989 and 1999. Over that same period, enrollment in for-profit institutions increased by 59 percent, compared with just seven percent enrollment growth in nonprofit institutions (Kelly, 2001, July). The landscape of for-profit higher education includes DeVry, Inc., with 56,000 students and 70 campuses and centers; ITT Educational Services, Inc., with 31,000 students at its over 70 campuses nationwide; and Strayer Education, Inc., with more than 14,000 students on its 20 campuses.

Without question, however, the giant of the for-profit higher education world is the University of Phoenix. One commentator asserted that the Apollo Group, the university's parent company, has "awakened the marketplace to the economic potential of postsecondary education" (Goldstein, 1998, July, p. 448). Founded in 1976, the University of Phoenix is the nation's largest private, accredited university, enrolling over 125,000 students, and boasting over 116 campuses nationwide. The Apollo Group reported fiscal 2001 profits of $108 million and projected revenues of up to $1.285 billion for fiscal year 2003 (Apollo, 2002; CNN, 2002, August 29a). Over the past five years, the company's stock price has risen over 220 percent (CNN, 2002, August 29b).

Reflecting the potential of the online education marketplace, the first year after its stock was offered to the public, the University of Phoenix Online, an Apollo Group spin-off, increased enrollments by 81 percent, revenue by 76 percent, and saw its stock price rise from $9.33 to $40.13 (Apollo, 2002). Analysts have lauded the company's "resilience to economic weakness, consistent business model, [and] attractive growth rates" (Briefing, 2001). Phoenix Online realized $31.8 million in profits in fiscal year 2001, an 82 percent increase over the previous year, and enrolled over 29,000 students (Apollo, 2002). For fiscal year 2003, the company projected revenues of up to $495 million (CNN, 2002, August 29a).

The stand-alone for-profit university is not the only story. Traditional nonprofit universities have also partnered with for-profit companies to offer online courses. The most prominent example is UNext, a company founded with $110 million, largely provided by Michael Milkin, the junk bond king and convicted felon. UNext partnered with such higher education notables as Stanford University, Columbia University, and the University of Chicago to deliver courses created by these institutions over the Internet. Columbia was guaranteed a minimum return of $20 million and, at the time, hoped to make much more in the company's anticipated stock offering (Keegan, 2000, December). Unfortunately, UNext's success never materialized. Similar partnerships include the Global Education Network, which enlisted

Williams and Wellesley Colleges; AllLearn, which included Oxford, Stanford and Yale Universities; and Universitas 21, composed of 17 universities internationally, and recently called the "new 900-pound gorilla on the block" (Abeles, 2002, August 2).

Fueling the growth of online partnerships and consortia are the titanic numbers of students and corporations in the market for online education. According to a Merrill Lynch estimate, 2.2 million college students will take online courses in 2002, a 210 percent increase since 1998 (Konrad, 2001, March 6). The online education market was estimated to grow to $25.3 billion by 2003 from $3.6 billion in 1999 (Altschuler, 2001, August 5; Grimes, 2001). The biggest piece of this market, corporate online education, was projected to grow from $1.1 billion in 1999 to $11.4 billion in 2003—a 79 percent compound annual growth rate. Higher education's share of the online market was expected to grow to $7 billion in 2003 from $1.2 billion in 1999. Hoping to reap the rewards of this growth, investors pumped almost $3 billion into online education companies in 1999 and 2000 alone (Grimes, 2001). However, despite the reported opportunities in online education, none of the for-profit subsidiaries created in recent years has reported a profit and several have ceased operations, citing economic and financial woes. Controversy over the lack of return on investment has brewed on many campuses as constituents have become aware of the enormous resources invested (Hafner, 2002).

CHALLENGING TRADITION

Yet, there is more at stake in the creation of for-profit subsidiaries than just economic success or return on investment. The creation (and in several cases demise) of these companies has sparked controversy, with some faculty claiming that the culture of the academy is being irreparably altered as traditional models of shared governance are being replaced by a top-down, corporate style management, or by some hybrid. These subsidiary companies, created to market and deliver online education to both student and corporate audiences, are to many the embodiment of destructive trends at work. These trends—marked by increasing connections to business and a growing proclivity for market behavior—have some "fearful that the university's true educational mission is being compromised" (Simpson, 2001, p. 54). Others assert the growing need to "make sure that the university does not betray its educational values and objectives" (Croissant, 2001, p. 45), or worry that market-oriented activities will eventually "change the social role of higher education institutions" for the worse (Breneman, 2002, June 14, p. B7). On an even darker note, Stanley Ikenberry (2001, Spring) warned that "any serious weakening in the integrity of the [university] or any corruption of the academic culture could be its undoing" (p. 15). (See also Nelson, 1997; Slaughter, 2001; Slaughter & Leslie, 1997; Smith, 2000; Soley, 1995; Stankiewicz, 1986).

The clamor over commercialization has embroiled the academy. One professor asked, "What is the difference between Yahoo! or America Online and Columbia University? Less and less" (Katz, 2001, June 15, p. B7). A professor at Columbia worried that the university "appears to be a for-profit enterprise." Another stewed over the long-term effects of realizing significant income from market activities, worrying that these activities "will reduce the credibility of universities and will probably reduce the willingness of society to take care of these institutions" (Arenson, 2000, August 2, p. A25).

Though these concerns have lately come to a head, the challenge to universities posed by business influence was first recognized almost one hundred years ago, when Thorstein Veblen railed against the university as a "corporation of learning" and college presidents as "captains of erudition" (as quoted in Birnbaum, 2000, p. 17). Veblen asserted that "the intrusion of business principles into the universities goes to weaken and retard the pursuit of learning, and therefore to defeat the ends for which a university is maintained" (as quoted in Birnbaum, 2000, p. 17).

Since Veblen, the debate has picked up steam, generating a battle between the classroom and the boardroom, with "students and professors on one side, and university administrators and companies . . . on the other" (Noble, 1998, p. 1). Some critics have questioned the quality of the courses offered by both for-profit universities and the new partnerships, and labeled any educational institution with a .com in its Internet address a "potential rip-off" (Altschuler, 2001, August 5, p. 13), or "a Wal-Mart education" (Keegan, 2000, December, p. 1).

On the other side of the debate, as market forces increase, many scholars and leaders argue that the academy must adapt to new market-driven realities. One professor asserted that technology and new ways of delivering education could increase the number of students served as well as protect at-risk programs by improving the university's financial condition (Carnevale, 1999, October 22). In a challenge to higher education leaders, Klor de Alva (2000, March/April), then president of the University of Phoenix, exhorted them to "rethink the rules that govern higher education today" (p. 36) and stressed that "many of the risk-averse, traditional rules of higher education are beginning to appear not merely quaint but irrelevant or even downright absurd" (p. 34).

FOR-PROFIT SUBSIDIARIES

For-profit subsidiaries embody the controversy. Some faculty have charged that these subsidiaries enable trustees and administrators to circumvent the normal channels of governance (Carr, 2000a), leaving faculty "out of the [governance] loop" (Carr, 1999, p. A46), bypassed in the decision-making process (Abel, 2000b). Opponents argue that the speed and manner in which these companies have been created are antithetical to the tradition and culture of shared governance (Kezar, 2001), and that top-down, corporate style management is regrettably replacing traditional models of shared governance. As one professor commented, for-profit subsidiaries "put the standard rules of academic governance on [their] head" (Abel, 2000b, p. A21).

At Cornell University, where there was considerable furor from faculty over the creation of eCornell (the university's for-profit subsidiary), governance was a key issue. One faculty member asserted that "the principle concern is one of control" (Carr, 2000c). Professors, worried about the influence of investors in the company on the governance and operation of the university, were cognizant of the fact that the entity controlling the purse strings usually controls all else. University officials admitted that due to the typically slow pace of faculty governance, it was not "completely clear how faculty-governance bodies fit" in the governance of eCornell (p. A41). Faculty at Temple University shared these same concerns and were particularly incensed by the administration's apparent refusal to include faculty in the discussions that led to the creation of the university's for-profit subsidiary, Virtual Temple, which was later closed.

Faculty members protest the lack of clarity over ownership of online material, wonder how the quality of the educational experience will be evaluated and assured, and worry about the lack of interaction with students in online courses; ultimately they fear for their jobs. "If I duplicate myself online, why do you need me?" (Abel, 2000a, p. B1). One commentator predicted that faculty could eventually be seen as mere laborers and lose their traditional status and position in higher education:

> With the commoditization of instruction, [faculty] . . . become subject to all the pressures that have befallen production workers in other industries. . . . Like these others, their activity is being restructured in order to reduce their autonomy, independence, and control over their work. . . . In short, the new technology of education, . . . robs faculty of their knowledge and skills, their control over their working lives, the product of their labor, and, ultimately, their means of livelihood. (Noble, 1998, p. 6)

Though this surely overstates the danger, others have speculated that the for-profit subsidiary might bifurcate faculty into those who teach online and those who remain in the traditional classroom (Newman, 2000, June 7). Worries about faculty tenure and promotion in the face of an increasingly commercial academy are summarized by one commentator: "Will a marginal professor's central role in a commercial venture influence a decision to grant him tenure?" (Steiner, 2000, August 7, p. A22). Ultimately, many faculty are simply philosophically opposed to the for-profit organizational format; claimed one professor, "That is the part of it that is most disturbing and unsettling for the faculty" (Carr, 2000a, p. A47).

In the face of this controversy, many scholars have documented the ever-increasing convergence between the nonprofit and for-profit organizational forms (Goldstein, 1998, July; Minow, 2000, March 23; Ryan, 1999, January/February; Weisbrod, 1997). Yet while the distinctions between nonprofit organizations and for-profit companies have blurred, particularly in higher education, a marriage between the two can present significant challenges. Oster (1995) asserted that these arrangements often precipitate serious governance issues, particularly when a new governance structure is created apart from the parent organization:

> On average, the goods and services nonprofits provide are more difficult to measure; they operate subject to a nondistribution constraint; they depend on both donations and fees for service; they use more labor than most for-profits, and most of that labor is professional and often ideologically motivated. Organizations that broaden to include under their wings for-profit businesses may well find that the management of those businesses requires a very different strategy and structure than they have used in their core ventures. And, it is often quite difficult to maintain one structure for one part of the business and a second structure for the rest of the business. (p. 96)

To avoid these complications, as colleges and universities have embraced market values, they have adjusted their governance structures and processes accordingly (Carlson, 2000a; Van Der Werf & Blumenstyk, 2001; Zusman, 1999). These adjustments prompted one commentator to proclaim, "Universities themselves are beginning to look and behave like for-profit companies" (Press & Washburn, 2000, March, p. 46).

CULTURE AND VALUES

Ultimately, the controversy is about values. Richard Posner argued that commercialization has caused colleges and universities to "lose their souls" (Posner, 2002, June). Similarly, condemning the current trajectory of higher education, James Perley, chair of the American Association of University Professors, asserted that such practices will "destroy the tradition of higher education as a community of scholars" (as quoted in Wilms & Zell, 2002). Another commented, "Private money is spreading through universities like a stain—infecting independent institutions with commercial values" (Ahuja, 2001, May 7).

The controversy, which some call a crisis, (Giroux, 2001) is centered on the academy's way of life, beliefs and values, the language that is used, the way decisions are made and who makes them, what is taught, and how faculty do their work and are rewarded for it. Thus, for many, the debate is not about how colleges and universities will operate, but instead, the nature and essence of the academy. It is not just about how business will be done, but whether the reason and purpose for getting things done will be business.

Because the creation and operation of for-profit subsidiaries centers on whether these entities are congruent with the non-profit university's mission, values, and basic assumptions, organizational culture theory offers the most appropriate conceptual framework for this study. In fact, to use other plausible frameworks—e. g., rationalism, power theory, economic or political theory—would eclipse the pivotal point of contention, a clash of culture and values. It is through the lens of organizational culture that one can best examine the "fit" between for-profit activity and nonprofit higher education. The utility of using organizational culture has been proven in many prominent studies of higher education (See Birnbaum, 1988, 1992; Chaffee & Tierney, 1988; Clark, 1963, 1972; Dill, 2000; Tierney, 1991). In the business community, cultural perspectives have also been used widely to understand corporations (See Deal & Kennedy, 1982; Kanter, 1983; Kotter & Heskett, 1992; Ouchi, 1981; Peters & Waterman, 1982).

Coming to an "all-embracing" definition of organizational culture has been called "elusive," "downright slippery," (Kuh & Whitt, 2000, p. 160), and "difficult" (Christensen & Shu, 1999, p. 1). One writer termed the concept, "impossibly vague" (Becher, 1984, p. 166). A 1952 study reported 164 definitions of culture (Kuh & Whitt, 2000); over the past four decades this number has undoubtedly mushroomed. Scholars have defined culture in various ways:

> "a core set of assumptions, understandings, and implicit rules that govern day-to-day behavior in the workplace" (Deal & Kennedy, 1982, p. 4);

> "those elements of a group or organization that are most stable and least malleable" (Schein, 1992, p. 5);

> "a set of commonly held attitudes, values, and beliefs that guide the behavior of an organization's members" (Martin, 1985, p. 148); and

> "the way we do things around here" (Arnold & Capella, 1985, p. 32).

Another, crafted particularly for colleges and universities, reads:

> The collective, mutually shaping patterns of norms, values, practices, beliefs, and assumptions that guide the behavior of individuals and

> groups in an institute of higher education and provide a frame of refer-
> ence within which to interpret the meaning of events and actions on and
> off campus. (Kuh & Whitt, 1988, p. 13)

Though the preceding definitions and concepts of culture have merit, this
study adheres to the concept of culture as defined by Schein (1992), because
the for-profit subsidiaries were created as a solution to various internal and
external problems (as I will discuss in Chapter 2).

> A pattern of shared basic assumptions that the group learned as it solved
> its problems of external adaptation and internal integration, that has
> worked well enough to be considered valid and, therefore, to be taught
> to new members as the correct way to perceive, think, and feel in rela-
> tion to those problems. (p. 12)

Schein's focus on the problem solving and adaptive nature of culture makes
it particularly appropriate for this study. Each of the for-profit subsidiaries
in this study was struggling not only to be successful in the marketplace, but
also to forge an appropriate and effective relationship with its parent institution. Each company's leaders were particularly crucial to this process. As
these leaders worked to solve the company's internal and external problems,
they created the "particular cultural content" (p. 49) that was passed on to
new organizational members and solidified "as the correct way to perceive,
think, and feel" (p. 12). These actions and the resulting culture either
clashed or blended with the culture and values of the parent institution.
Thus, the creation and perpetuation of culture by the actions and beliefs of
organizational personnel and the socialization of new members are central
to this study and prominent in Schein's concept of culture.

Even Schein's definition, however, is not all-encompassing. It does not include an overt reference to the powerful effect culture has on action, though it
is implied that a person's perceptions, thoughts, and feelings ultimately guide
behavior. Schein (1992) recognizes that culture can have a powerful controlling
effect on organizational participants, even to the point of "explicitly manipu-
lating members" to act in line with cultural tenets (p. 13). In addition, an organization's culture shapes its policies, processes, and structure, and thereby
provides a foundation for governance (Masland, 1991). In fact, when an organization's cultural values are jeopardized or changed, the organization's view
of reality and appropriate actions are subsequently threatened and can even be
fundamentally altered (Kotter & Heskett, 1992; Schein, 1992). In this way, culture acts as a "mechanism of social control," exerting a powerful influence on
how organization members act, think, and feel (Schein, 1992 p. 13).

Schein (1992) characterized culture on three levels: artifacts—"visible organizational structures and processes"; espoused values—"strategies, goals, and philosophies of the organization"; and basic assumptions—"unconscious beliefs, perceptions, and feelings" (p. 17). Artifacts are easy to observe but often difficult to decipher, comprising the everyday trappings of the organization, including architecture, the layout of physical space, job titles and descriptions, governing bodies and committees, technology, products of the organization, myths and stories, and even attire (Harrison, 1994; Schein, 1992). Espoused values are discussed and even debated by organizational participants, but when these values are internalized, they can become basic assumptions. These assumptions then "are so taken for granted that someone who does not hold them is viewed as crazy and automatically dismissed" (Schein, 1992, p. 16). Basic assumptions are "neither confronted nor debated" and are largely resistant to change (p. 22); behavior out of line with these assumptions is unthinkable.

It is in basic assumptions and values that the corporation and the academy most differ (Schein, 1992). Higher education espouses the values of professional autonomy and academic freedom (Young, 1997). Beneath the espoused value of academic freedom reside several basic assumptions: the unfettered pursuit of "truth"; the discovery of knowledge for its own sake, for social good, and for public benefit; the sharing, rather than hoarding, of knowledge (Austin, 1990; Kuh & Whitt, 1988), and, particularly among faculty, the notion that the institution is a "community of scholars who work together to govern the institution" (Austin, 1990, p. 62; see also Millett, 1962). Shared governance is a basic assumption and central tenet of the academy.

Conversely, basic assumptions in for-profit organizations include capitalism, the pursuit of profit, the discovery of knowledge for competitive advantage, and the patenting and hoarding of knowledge for commercial purposes. Additionally, the for-profit sector prizes market-oriented decision-making, efficient operations, cost reduction, and accountability for results. In contrast to governance by a community of scholars, for-profit corporations are typically governed by a clear hierarchy (Oster, 1995). Colleges are ideally collegial in nature, whereas corporations are managerial (Millett, 1962).

A particularly prominent difference between the nonprofit and for-profit sectors is the absence of the profit motive in the academy. Because the pursuit of profit is not an issue for the nonprofit college or university, students, parents, and the general public can trust the work of the disinterested scholar and his institution (Weisbrod, 1988).

Drucker (1989) articulated a key distinction between governance in for-profits and nonprofits, which underscores the cultural incongruencies: "The businesses I work with start their planning with financial returns. The non-profits start with the performance of their missions" (p. 89). Oster (1995) asserted that a non-profit's mission and organizational values are "quite central to management in a way that it is often not in the corporate world" (p. 12). However, many proclaim that universities should be run more like businesses (Carlin, 1999; Mahoney, 1997; Myers, 2001; Sowell, 1998, September 7; Willis, 2001) and argue that nonprofit colleges and universities should shift their governance practices from the traditional shared governance of the academy, which some term "unworkable" (Ruch, 2001, p. 153), to the more hierarchical and market-oriented practices of the corporate world (Knight, 2001, March). This shift, which impacts the traditional values and mission of the nonprofit university, is at the heart of the controversy over the creation of for-profit subsidiaries in nonprofit higher education.

Chapter Two

Creating the Subsidiaries: Unsolved Problems and Multiple Messages

University administrators and trustees certainly face a formidable litany of problems: declining governmental support at both the state and federal level, rising costs, increasing competition for the best and brightest students, growing concerns over institutional rankings, bitter ideological battles over the direction and substance of the curriculum, pressure from governmental agencies for more accountability, and expectations from constituents that higher education not only be a substantial contributor to the economy's health but also assure individuals attractive positions in that economy. These pressures, coupled with the success of for-profit higher education companies, motivated many college officials to consider the Internet and the corporate sector as a possible antidote. The for-profit subsidiary appeared to be a solution to almost everyone's problems.

In this chapter I discuss the for-profit subsidiary as an attractive solution to a set of internal and external problems identified by administrators and trustees of each parent institution. The next four subsections describe briefly the creations of the four subsidiaries, as well as relevant history for each parent institution. I then consider organizational choice in higher education, particularly at "organized anarchies," and present data on why the subsidiaries were created and whether the subsidiaries in fact solved the problems, as intended. Finally, the chapter concludes with a discussion of how administrators used a double set of messages to articulate the reason for the subsidiary.

CREATING THE SUBSIDIARIES

Babson Interactive, LLC

Babson College formed Babson Interactive, LLC in August 2000, and named Thomas Moore, then dean of Babson's Graduate School of Business and School of Executive Education, as chief executive officer. Touted as an appropriate response to the expanded distance-learning market, the move was heralded by the media as an example of Babson's commitment to entrepreneurship (Wood, 2000, September 6, p. 2).

The creation of the company seemed to fit within Babson College's focus on business entrepreneurship. In fact, Babson is recognized as a leader in teaching entrepreneurship through its innovative curriculum at the undergraduate and graduate level that incorporates a cross-disciplinary approach to teaching business and the liberal arts. Babson's MBA program focuses on entrepreneurial leadership. But entrepreneurship is not only what Babson teaches, it is also what the College practices and promotes. First-year students participate in the Foundation Management Experience, a year-long program, funded by the College, that enables students to start and run their own businesses. *U.S. News & World Report* (USNews, 2003) recently ranked Babson College number one among business schools in teaching entrepreneurship.

Babson College has always been entwined with business. On September 3, 1919, Roger Babson founded the Babson Institute with 27 students. A millionaire entrepreneur and first president of the Institute, Babson's success in business was due to his entrepreneurship, a skill that he wanted to instill in students. A College history recounts: "Roger Ward Babson's idea of a rigorous and pragmatic business education that always embraced the new while maintaining the traditional values of work and service has been the hallmark of Babson College." (Babson, 2001, p. 1)

Table 2–1. Institutional Profile—Babson College

Babson College	
Founded	1919
Location	Wellesley, Massachusetts
Control	Private
Undergraduate enrollment (2001)	1,701
Admissions acceptance rate (2001)	35%
SAT scores (25–75 percentile) (2002)	1170–1330
Annual operating budget (1999)	$105.7 million
Current endowment (1999)	$147.3 million
U.S. News & World Report ranking (2003)	ranked #1 in business entrepreneurship

In accordance with Babson's philosophy, the Institute's first programs were aimed to meet the needs of students who wanted a very focused business education but who also wanted to spend as little time out of the workforce as possible. Intensive training in finance, production, and distribution was completed in just one year rather than four. Due to the pace of the program, it was assumed that students would receive training in the liberal arts elsewhere. The curriculum focused on practical experience rather than traditional classroom lectures—students worked in groups, gave presentations to each other, toured local businesses and manufacturing facilities, and spoke often with business managers and executives. Babson's ideal was to prepare students "to enter their chosen careers as executives," rather than as anonymous members of the work force (Babson, 2001, p. 5). In line with this objective, the Institute became a "simulated business environment," with students wearing professional attire, keeping regular business hours, and even punching in and out on a time clock. Each student had a desk equipped with the era's business essentials—typewriter, telephone, adding machine, and Dictaphone—and each student had a secretary to type his assignments and correspondence.

Over time, Babson Institute's programs developed from a one-year certificate in business administration into more traditional academic offerings. In 1934, the Institute offered a two-year certificate, and in 1944, the Commonwealth of Massachusetts approved a three-year Bachelor of Science program. The Institute awarded its first bachelor's degree in 1947. In 1951, the first cohort of Master's of Business Administration students was admitted, and in 1961, an evening MBA program was formed. In 1969, two years after the death of Roger Babson, the Institute officially became Babson College (Babson, 2001).

With this history as backdrop, in early 1999, it became increasingly clear to both trustees and administrators of Babson College that competition in graduate business education was heating up, driven mainly by new distance-learning programs. The growth of institutions like the University of Phoenix and Jones International University posed little threat to Babson, but the announcement of the creation of a Global MBA, and later a Cross-Continent MBA, online educational programs begun by Duke University's Fuqua School of Business, raised the stakes for Babson administrators. When business schools at the University of Florida and the University of North Carolina also announced distance-learning initiatives, this uneasiness intensified. Moore commented: "We started to take notice. Here was a group of top 20 schools all getting into this game and we decided we better look at it very carefully."

With concern building, Babson's vice president for academic affairs formed a committee, commissioned by the board of trustees. The committee, which included Moore, two faculty members, the college's chief financial officer, and an outside consultant, was to explore the opportunities and challenges posed by distance learning. This committee was charged to think strategically about Babson's response to the new competitive environment and directed to present its recommendations at a board of trustees' retreat in early February 2000. Several trustees were actively interested in the online education issue. Two trustees in particular, Craig Benson, the former chief executive of a major business software firm, and John Landry, the former chief technologist for Lotus, "were pushing very, very hard that we needed to be in [the distance-learning] space," said Moore. Following the presentation, the trustees gave the president a mandate to prepare a plan for entering online education by the next board meeting. To meet this mandate, the committee prepared a proposal to create a separate for-profit entity to deliver distance education. The purpose was twofold: defensive—to protect Babson's evening MBA program—and offensive—to create new corporate-related degree and non-degree programs.

In March 2000, President Leo Higdon approached the board for approval of Babson Interactive, but did not ask for a formal board vote (even though a majority of the board reportedly supported the move) because he planned to use $2.5 million of discretionary money to fund the venture. With the tacit approval of the board's executive committee, Babson Interactive was created, without formal discussion or approval by the faculty.

Duke Corporate Education, Inc.

Determined to take its place among the nation's best universities and guided by presidents who were called "outrageously ambitious," Duke University has sought, as one of these presidents asserted, to "shape our own destiny, in our own way, in our own place" (Sanford, 1984). Trustees of the university noted in 1924 that Duke had had three names and two locations and that "it changes again to meet changing conditions" (King, 2002). The premier university in the South, and considered by many as one of the top institutions in America, Duke University enrolled almost 12,000 students in fall 2002, and had an annual operating budget of over $2 billion. In its 2003 rankings, *US News & World Report* (USNews, 2003) ranked Duke tied for 4th among national universities.

Table 2–2. Institutional Profile—Duke University

Duke University	
Founded	1838 (Union Institute); 1859 (Trinity College); 1924 (Duke University)
Location	Durham, North Carolina
Control	Private
Undergraduate enrollment (2002)	5,916
Admissions acceptance rate (2002)	23%
SAT scores (25–75 percentile) (2002)	1320–1500
Annual operating budget (2002)	$2.417 billion
Current endowment (2002)	$2.441 billion
U.S. News & World Report ranking (2003)	Ranked #4 (tie) among National Universities Doctoral

Duke has seen many changes since its founding as the Union Institute, in 1838, by Methodist and Quaker families in rural North Carolina. Since then, the institution has been called Normal College (1851), Trinity College (1859), and finally, Duke University (1924). From its rural beginnings, Trinity College was moved to Durham in 1892, in order to take advantage of the benefits of an urban setting. In 1894, Washington Duke, a prosperous and influential member of the Durham community, became interested in Trinity and established an endowment of $300,000. With this support, and by hiring a young and able faculty from Johns Hopkins, Columbia, and other Northern universities, Trinity developed into one of the finest liberal arts colleges in the South.

In 1924, James B. Duke, son of Washington Duke, established the Duke Endowment to support a university named in his father's honor. Duke University grew rapidly, adding a graduate school, a school of religion, a medical school and hospital, a school of nursing, and a school of forestry within a 14-year span. In addition, the Law School was reorganized and the department of engineering was established as a separate school. In 1938, Duke became a member of the Association of American Universities. The growth of Duke has been called the "greatest transformation in [the shortest] period of time . . . in the history of higher education in the South" (King, 2002). James B. Duke's last desire was fulfilled in 1969, when the School of

Business Administration, later named the Fuqua School of Business, was established.

In its short history, the Fuqua School of Business has demonstrated a spirit and flair for innovation. Since enrolling its first class of 12 MBA students in 1970, Fuqua had solidified its place next to Harvard, Stanford, and Wharton as one of the world's top business schools. Between 1994 and 2000, Fuqua had climbed six spots in the *Business Week* annual ranking of business schools; in 2002, it ranked fifth. In 2000, *Business Week* reported that Fuqua had "taken the B-school world by storm" (Merritt, 2000). With a campus in Frankfurt, Germany and other international offerings, the school was pursuing an aggressive global expansion strategy designed to fulfill its mission "to provide the highest quality education for business and academic leaders."

Fuqua had become a major player in the education of business executives and particularly in the custom executive education business. Dean Rex Adams and Associate Dean Blair Sheppard considered customized executive education the key to a strong future because of its ability to reach into the corridors of the corporate world in ways that expanded Fuqua's influence and prestige. The School had generated annual revenues of as much as $14 million in this market and competed favorably against the likes of Stanford, Harvard, and Wharton. In 2000, Fuqua was ranked fifth globally in executive education by the *Financial Times*. A central feature of Fuqua's new approach was innovative use of technology that enabled delivery of customized courses or modules via the Internet.

In 1997, Fuqua faculty and administrators realized that the success of executive education—particularly the customized business—was altering the School's culture. As executive education grew, a gap developed between Fuqua's traditional, and intensifying, research-based culture and its newer focus on executive education, which involved professors who adhered to a more "clinical" bent in their work. "Born out of a schism," as one professor stated, Duke Corporate Education (Duke CE) was created to heal this growing rift.

In Fall 1999, a committee composed of both faculty and administrators, including Sheppard, released a report that proposed two strategic alternatives for executive education:

1. Expand custom executive education, within the school's existing organizational structure, to meet market demand
2. Create a for-profit subsidiary responsible for managing custom executive education.

John Gallagher, a Fuqua administrator, described the reaction of some faculty to the notion of expanding executive education within the school's existing structure:

> If you thought that executive education was inherently undesirable to begin with and produced the wrong teaching and research incentives for faculty, then certainly putting it on steroids and quadrupling the size of the business seemed like a really, really bad idea.

Under the second proposal, faculty were essentially unwilling to risk the asset the program had become and the income stream it generated for the School. Eventually, both proposals were tabled by the faculty and essentially killed. Sheppard's reading of faculty reaction to the committee's report was clear and unequivocal. "It was fair to say," he commented, "that this report was the least-well-received document that I had ever been party to creating."

However, in June 2000, with a new provost and under the threat of Sheppard's departure, the issue resurfaced. This time, Sheppard had the support of Duke's central administration, who lobbied intensely on his behalf. With assurances from the central administration and a deal that guaranteed a $12 million annual payment to Fuqua from the company, Fuqua's faculty overwhelmingly approved the creation of Duke Corporate Education.

The idea for the company had risen partly from the success of Fuqua's initial forays into online education. Fuqua had proven the advantages and potential financial rewards from online education through the success of its Global Executive MBA program. In the program, students were required to spend 11 weeks in residential classes held at sites around the world, with the remainder of the degree delivered via interactive Internet technology. To deliver this program, Fuqua had created a sophisticated technological platform that could also be used to deliver customized education to corporations on a scale that had not been done before.

Sheppard was named the company's CEO and negotiated a deal with a venture capital company, which was all but secured in late 2000 when the market changed significantly for Internet-based companies. The estimated worth of Duke CE thus plummeted by 50 percent. The drop in value meant that Duke would have to surrender a greater percentage of the ownership of the company in return for investment capital. Unwilling to give up a significantly greater share of Duke CE than planned, yet committed to not use academic resources to finance the company, Duke administrators guaranteed a line of credit that would fund the company until alternative financing could be secured. (For a complete description of the founding of Duke Corporate Education see Bleak, 2001, June.)

Fathom Knowledge Network, Inc.

Columbia University, a member of the prestigious Ivy League and considered one of the top universities in the world, was founded in 1754, by King George II as King's College. Today the university enrolls over 23,000 students and boasts an endowment of over $4 billion. It is the oldest institution of higher education in the state of New York and fifth oldest in the United States (Facets, 2001).

In its original charter, King's College was charged with giving future leaders of society an education designed to "enlarge the Mind, improve the Understanding, polish the whole Man, and qualify them to support the brightest Characters in all the elevated stations in life" (Columbia, 1999). Under these ambitious goals, a medical school was established in 1767 and the first M.D. degrees in America were awarded in 1770.

Closed during the American Revolution, the college reopened in 1784 with a new name, Columbia. Columbia College grew rapidly over the next 100 years and in 1896 declared itself a university. In that same year, the university dedicated its new Morningside Heights campus (Facets, 2001).

Under the leadership of Nicholas Murray Butler, from 1902 to 1945, Columbia emerged as one of the nation's preeminent institutions. Its faculty were renowned for their groundbreaking research and scholarship, and Columbia became, in the words of one alumnus, a place of "doubled magic," where "the best things of the moment were outside the rectangle of Columbia; the best things of all human history and thought were inside the rectangle" (Columbia, 1999).

Table 2–3. Institutional Profile—Columbia University

Columbia University	
Founded	1754 (as King's College); 1784 (reopened after Revolutionary War as Columbia College)
Location	Manhattan, New York City
Control	Private
Undergraduate enrollment (2002)	7,054
Admissions acceptance rate (2002)	12%
SAT scores (25–75 percentile) (2002)	1320–1510
Annual operating budget (2001)	$1.722 billion
Current endowment (2001)	$4.324 billion
US News & World Report ranking (2003)	Ranked #10 among National Universities—Doctoral

In March 1998, Columbia University's Board of Trustees, in an extended board discussion, which included some members of the Columbia faculty and its senior administrators, considered how the University could protect its brand name. The discussion, at a day and a half retreat, came on the heels of a report from a multi-school faculty working group that had been charged to "explore how the University might participate in the digital media arena in ways that reflect and express our core intellectual and educational values." George Rupp, Columbia University's president, specifically mentioned competition from for-profit educational enterprises and publishing companies that were making their products available online, " . . . [W]e are not completely insulated from the forces at work in these markets and are therefore well advised to be vigilant in protecting Columbia interests while we are also both prudent and creative in projecting the Columbia identity into this domain." (Rupp, 2000, February 29).

From the board's deliberations, a four-prong strategy emerged: 1) experiments with the use of new media for teaching and learning, funded by the central administration but nested in individual schools and colleges; 2) creating the Columbia Center for New Media Teaching and Learning, an organization to assist faculty in producing digital educational materials and online courses; 3) establishing Columbia Media Enterprises, which was formerly called Morningside Ventures, an organization to explore how the University could increase its outreach efforts by "developing extensions of the university" into the online education marketplace; and 4) creating digital media courses or course segments for use by business ventures the University had partnered with, including UNext.com and Cognitive Arts, Ind. This strategy was centered on the idea of "[serving] the university through the maximization of intellectual property" and to "take advantage of technology" (Shea, 2001, September 16, p. W25).

Columbia Media Enterprises and The Center for New Media Teaching and Learning, the key initiatives in this overall digital media strategy, were to provide a place within Columbia for professors to develop and market educational products. This strategy was advanced on three fronts: internal development and innovation, entrepreneurial outreach, and market positioning. Rupp assigned Michael Crow, Columbia's executive vice provost, with overall responsibility for coordinating and implementing the strategy, which Provost Jonathan Cole termed a "large experiment or series of experiments."

Perhaps the biggest experiment of all was the creation of Fathom, a for-profit subsidiary legally spun-off from Columbia in May 2000 and funded with $18.7 million. Faculty were not consulted directly regarding the creation of Fathom and the initial funding for the company was from money that fell outside Columbia's normal budgetary process and thus outside faculty review.

The idea for Fathom originated in Morningside Ventures and was the brainchild of Ann Kirschner. Envisioned as a means to advance Columbia's entrepreneurial outreach and market position, Fathom was created as a consortium that would deliver educational materials over the Internet. Fathom's partners included the British Library, the London School of Economics and Political Science, the New York Public Library, Cambridge University Press, and the Smithsonian Institution's National Museum of Natural History. Because Columbia wanted to retain complete control of the company, none of its partner institutions contributed to funding Fathom.

NYUonline, Inc.

New York University (NYU) is one of the largest private, non-profit universities in the United States and one of only 27 private institutions with membership in the prestigious Association of American Universities. The University has an undergraduate student body of 18,628, and a total enrollment of almost 60,000 students, hailing from all 50 states and 120 foreign countries. These students are served by more than 2,600 faculty. With an annual operating budget of over $1 billion, NYU maintains fourteen schools and colleges, offers over 2,500 different courses and occupies six major centers in Manhattan, as well as two satellite locations in adjoining counties.

Table 2–4. Institutional Profile—New York University

New York University	
Founded	1831
Location	Manhattan, New York
Control	Private
Undergraduate enrollment (2002)	18,628
Admissions acceptance rate (2002)	32%
SAT scores (25–75 percentile) (2002)	1230–1420
Annual operating budget (1999)	$1.356 billion
Current endowment (1999)	$1.036 billion
US News & World Report) ranking (2003)	Ranked #35 among National Universities—Doctoral

The history of NYU has been referred to as the "Miracle on Washington Square" (NYUToday, 2000, October 26, p. 1). One commentator called the founding and growth of the University "a genuine cliffhanger, the tale of an institution and its leaders struggling to survive" (p. 1). Established in 1831, NYU aspired to help New York City become the "London of America" (NYU, 2001) by creating a new type of American university. It was to be a "national university" that, according to its first president, would provide a "rational and practical education for all" (NYU, 2000). This education would not only include the traditional subjects of law, medicine, and the study of Greek and Latin, but would also serve aspiring "merchants, mechanics, farmers, manufacturers, architects, and civil engineers . . . with equal privileges and equal advantages" (NYU, 2001). The founder's overriding vision was that the University would help to "enlarge the opportunities of education" (Handbook, 2001, May 10, p. 1).

NYU's history is replete with stories of how its leaders maintained, "a firm and focused grasp on the University's direction, and [had] the courage to make critical, even painful choices, in the quest for a secure and healthy future" (p. 1). In fact, the University's first building, a Gothic structure modeled after King's College in Cambridge, England, was constructed even before the money to pay for it had been completely secured (NYU, 2001). One of the "painful choices" made by the University's leaders in response to a fiscal crisis in the late 1960's was to sell part of the campus. An NYU historian commented:

> . . . There is an entrepreneurial thread that runs through the University's history. In times of great challenge, instead of saying, 'Well, we're facing this insurmountable crisis so it looks like we'll have to close,' there seems to have always been a core group that has come together and, instead, said, 'We're facing this problem, what can we do about it? Let's find a way to deal with it.' (NYUToday, 2000, October 26, p. 2)

Consistent with this history, in early 1998, Gerald Heeger, dean of NYU's School of Continuing and Professional Studies (SCPS)[1], proposed to the University's central administration and board the idea of creating a for-profit subsidiary. Following a series of meetings between the board and senior administration to vet Heeger's proposal, the board of trustees approved an initial investment of $21.5 million in NYUonline and formally created the company in October 1998. Because the new venture's funding was seen as an investment of the University's endowment, this decision did not receive faculty consultation or comment, beyond discussions with the deans of NYU's schools.

David Finney, Heeger's successor as dean of SCPS[2,] and several other NYU administrators managed NYUonline during its first year of operation. In January 2000, the company offered its first online courses leading to a Certificate in Management Training (Letterman, 1999, October 20). In that same month, NYUonline hired Gordon Macomber, a veteran media publisher and e-commerce executive, as president and CEO.

ORGANIZATIONAL CHOICE IN HIGHER EDUCATION

To examine more closely how and why each of these institutions made the decision to start a for-profit subsidiary for online education, it is useful to explore first the broader context of decision-making in colleges and universities. Alternately described as academic communities, collegiums, bureaucracies, political arenas, and businesses, the academy is nothing if not enigmatic. One of the most fascinating descriptions of the academy is as an "organized anarchy," where organizational goals are problematic or ambiguous, technology is unclear, and participation in governance and decision-making is fluid (Cohen & March, 1986).

As a result of these general properties, Cohen and March (1986) characterize a university as an organization that "does not know what it is doing" (p. 3), aptly exhibited in the process by which choices are made. There are several metaphorical "streams" flowing through a university—streams only tangentially connected to each other that consist of problems, solutions, decision-makers, and choice opportunities. "Problems are the unresolved concerns of people within the institution" (Birnbaum, 1988, p. 160), which, importantly, "may not be resolved when choices are made" (Cohen & March, 1986, p. 82). Solutions are someone's product and flow through the institution looking for problems to which they might be the answer. In universities, often the problem to be solved is not well-defined until the solution is identified. Participants involved in a decision "come and go" (p. 82), taking part fluidly depending on the attributes of the decision opportunity. Choice opportunities are circumstances, like meetings or budget approvals, in which an organization might be expected to produce a decision. These four streams converge in a process that has been called "garbage can" decision-making, where problems, solutions, and participants combine, seemingly randomly and at times irrationally, at choice opportunities to produce decisions. In sum, the university has been termed "a collection of choices looking for problems, issues and feelings looking for decision situations in which they might be aired, solutions looking for issues to which they might be the answer, and decision makers looking for work" (Cohen & March, 1986, p. 81).

In the absence of clear goals and a known technology, academic administrators—"decision makers looking for work"—often identify a favorite and sometimes trendy solution—"an answer actively looking for a question" (Cohen & March, 1986, p. 82)—and proclaim it to be the response to a specific issue or a complicated conundrum. When the solution, problem, and choice opportunity all come together in an environment fertile for decisions, these solutions will prevail. For the institutions in this study, the solution to various financial, strategic and organizational imperatives was the creation of the for-profit subsidiary.

SOLVING FINANCIAL PROBLEMS

How do we earn money?

Colleges and universities seem to be eternally in need of more money. One academic asserted that the academy possesses "a genetic predisposition against cost cutting and an incessant thirst for revenue" (Chait, 2000). The cost of providing a quality college education continues to increase, far outstripping inflation. Between 1958 and 1989, the cost of equipping a laboratory in the physical or natural sciences rose 2.5 times faster than inflation, and over the past twenty years, the cost of purchasing other essential goods and services also outpaced inflation (Benjamin, Carroll, Jacobi, Krop, & Shires, 1993, p. 19). Since 1979, faculty salaries, a major component of higher education's costs, grew at an average annual rate that exceeded inflation (Benjamin et al., 1993, p. 19). Between 1975 and 1990, student services costs increased 48 percent at public institutions and 78 percent at private institutions. Over this same period, instructional costs rose 30 percent (Tierney, 1999, p. 3). Though many have condemned what they see as unnecessary spending in higher education, students have come to demand it: "In a competitive market, "customers" expect particular resources, such as child care, computer terminals, and so on, and if the college does not have them, then the consumers will take their money elsewhere." (Tierney, 1999, p. 3)

As the cost of providing education has risen, many have decried the subsequent rise in tuition, yet most do not realize that tuition seldom covers the actual cost; at some institutions, often the highest rated, the proportion of costs covered by tuition is as low as 20 percent (See Winston, 1996, November; Winston, 1997, September/October; Winston & Yen, 1995, July). The remaining 80 percent must come from somewhere, and as costs rise administrators are increasingly called on to meet the shortfall (Smith, 2000).

The need for increased revenue is compounded by administrators' hesitancy to cut costs, which can provoke fierce institutional politics, unpopular decisions, and dissatisfaction with management. This frequently persuades academic administrators that the solution to a budgetary problem lies on the revenue side:

> While nearly all administrators minimally have to pay lip service to controlling costs, most would much prefer to resolve their economic problems by increasing revenues. Administrators of every type would rather expand their empire than diminish it. (Smith, 2000, p. 64)

As expenditures have risen, some forms of revenue have declined. Between 1987 and 1992, state appropriations per full-time student fell 13 percent (Tierney, 1999, p. 4). A recent RAND report concluded that higher education has been severely underfunded by the government "since the mid-1970's" (p. 3), and the future for government funding does not look bright (Zusman, 1999). Even as tuition was rising, colleges increased their financial aid budgets in order to maintain enrollments, which effectively reduced net revenue.

The opportunity to tap an additional source of revenue was a key reason for creating for-profit subsidiaries. Harvey Stedman, then provost of NYU, frankly asserted, "if they say it's not about the money, it's about the money." "This is all about money. Because of the way it runs, the way you make money and then how it creates value. You can issue stock and equity. People want to own it. And you could make a trillion dollars because it's IPOs and dot com stuff." When asked the rationale behind the creation of NYUonline, one top administrator frankly commented, "We need money." Another cited the potential the company had to bolster the university's endowment through a public stock offering. David Finney, dean of NYU's School of Continuing and Professional Studies, commented:

> It was clear that if the university was to play in [the online learning] sandbox at all, we had to at least get in. If we stood on the sidelines there were no possibilities. And if we got in and invested some amount of money, and . . . if we came up with a strategy and a company that happened to hit . . . we were all going to be better off.

Of course, the NYU administration was not alone in envisioning dollar signs when considering creating a for-profit subsidiary. The notion that a for-profit subsidiary could make an institution "better off" financially, to one degree or another, was a common thread in each case. The provost at Duke University termed the creation of Duke Corporate Education, "an opportunity to put the business school on a better footing, and to make some money" for the university as a whole. George Rupp, president of Columbia, commented that one of the reasons for creating Fathom as a for-profit entity was that "it might indeed generate revenue." A former vice president at Babson and a tenured member of the faculty, Allen Cohen, confirmed that one of the explanations for the creation of Babson Interactive was the potential to "bring in lots of money."

Where do we get the necessary capital?

In addition to the enticement of an additional revenue stream for the university, the need for start-up capital favored the for-profit model. Online learning requires a different business model than traditional classroom-based instruction. In classroom-based instruction, revenues are matched to expenses—students pay tuition, which is then used to pay faculty and cover other instructional expenses (Goldstein, 2000a). The work performed matches the services provided. Technology-based instruction is profoundly different. Online courses can be extremely expensive to develop—a high-quality course can cost as much as $500,000 to $1 million—and courses must be created before any tuition revenues are collected. This creates a substantial need for working capital in advance of revenues (Goldstein, 2000a, 2000b).

Historically, colleges and universities had four options to access capital: (1) obtaining philanthropic donations, (2) assuming debt, (3) tapping institutional reserves and current revenues, or (4) raising prices while lowering costs (Goldstein, 2000b). However, at the height of the dot-com gold rush, investor capital was quite plentiful and many institutions chose this route.

Finney articulated the need for capital at NYUonline, "At that time, it looked like putting a high quality course online in any sort of a sophisticated format was going to be very expensive, so there was a need to secure a lot of capital." Rupp and Michael Crow, Columbia's executive vice provost, cited the ability to raise capital from sources outside the university as a key reason for the incorporation of Fathom as a for-profit company. As Crow stated, "it would take several hundred million dollars to ultimately make Fathom work." Ann Kirschner, Fathom's CEO, noted the expensive nature of the planned activities at Fathom and the absolute necessity to be able to raise capital via the for-profit organizational structure. Moore argued that the for-profit organizational structure was necessary to give Babson Interactive the ability to raise capital "outside the normal budgetary process." Michael Fetters, Babson College's vice president for academics, concurred that the for-profit structure was "the only way that we could fund the development of the product." Wanda Wallace, a founder of Duke CE and former vice president for executive education at the Fuqua School of Business, commented that Duke CE's technology and software platform needed to be "built in advance of the sale" and thus required capital investment prior to revenue generation. John Payne, an assistant dean at the Fuqua School, stated that capital from outside the university was needed to allow Duke CE "to build and expand faster than we might be able to do on our own dollar."

SOLVING COMPETITIVE PROBLEMS

How do we compete favorably with other institutions?

Competition from peer institutions has become a prime motivator for colleges and universities (Bailey, Badway, & Gumport, 2001; Newman, 2002, April 26; Newman & Couturier, 2001, June; Winston & Zimmerman, 2000, May-June). As competition to attract the best students and faculty increased, many institutions experimented with alternatives to traditional academic structures and arrangements (Blum, 2002; Brett, Gibson, & Smilor, 1991; Collis, 2001; Ruch, 1999, February). These experiments included for-profit subsidiaries, partnerships between universities and corporations, as well as other connections and affiliations with business and government (Collis, 2001; Etzkowitz, Webster, & Healey, 1998; Til, 2000).

The need to meet the competition was a prominent reason for the creation of the four subsidiaries. When asked about the launch of Babson Interactive, Moore mentioned the distance-learning initiatives of competitor universities and the pressure that created for Babson to "[get] into this game." Babson administrators sought to "understand the environment," to know the "players" entering the MBA distance-learning market, and to think strategically about the opportunities and challenges the Internet posed. Said Fetters, "We felt that distance learning technology . . . was truly a disruptive technology[3], and that we had to move quicker than educational institutions typically move."

Payne underscored Duke's need to respond to competition in an unconventional way.

> "To really move ahead, we had to somehow break the boundaries of the game—go outside the normal rules. . . . We couldn't wait for the world to come to Durham, we had to go to the world."

At Columbia, Rupp emphasized the need to respond to competition, but also "to make sure Columbia was positioned in what was thought to be a major change in the educational landscape," i.e., the Internet. Rupp asserted that Fathom was needed to "make sure we were players as this new form of delivery . . . was developed."

How do we protect and retain intellectual property?

These subsidiaries were also created as part of a defensive strategy to protect course materials and other educational products, referred to collectively as intellectual property. Hanley (2002, September-October) asserted, "Intellectual property is what happens to ideas once they have been converted into exclusive, saleable commodities, subject to the same legal and economic principles as any other form of property."

Because faculty create intellectual property, one rationale for the subsidiary was the university's desire to have faculty teach online within the institution rather than for other universities and competitors eager to entice well-known professors to deliver content and license intellectual property. Administrators wanted to provide a mechanism for the distribution and marketing of faculty expertise that satisfied an individual professor's entrepreneurial needs within the confines and "businesses" of the university.

This move was motivated to some degree by the "Arthur Miller problem." A professor at Harvard Law School, Miller agreed to provide Concord University School of Law, an online institution, with videotaped lectures. Harvard asserted that Miller had violated university policy; however, Miller argued his rights by countering that he "doesn't teach at the [Concord] law school or even interact with its students, in person or online" (Carnevale & Young, 1999, p. A45).

Though this incident was specific to Harvard, many institutions saw a harbinger. One commentator predicted that "someday, all law students will study from Arthur R. Miller" (Leibowitz, 2000, p. A45). Administrators were concerned that their own faculty would sell course material to a competitor or to a for-profit company. In both cases, the economic benefits would bypass the university. (See also Matrix, 2001 for a discussion of the Arthur Miller case and the related controversy over intellectual property rights.)

For-profit subsidiaries allowed administrators to take the offensive prior to an Arthur Miller problem by: (1) compensating faculty for the use of course material, and (2), providing a vehicle for faculty to benefit financially while under the university's umbrella. Harvey Stedman proclaimed, "We didn't want to get into the [Arthur Miller] position. . . . I didn't want that mess." Rupp agreed:

The idea was that if we all worked together, we were going to be better off than if we just had a star system where people were picked off and they made out well, but there was nothing that came back to benefit the university—this is the Arthur Miller problem.

Kirschner commented that the Columbia trustees "were very concerned about an Arthur Miller scenario."

It was critical to get ahead of that and figure out what a structure would be so [trustees and administrators] would have a good story to tell faculty. This would be, 'Look, the university has in place mechanisms and resources for you to use to develop either specific commercial programs or just other ways to develop intellectual properties.'

How do we attract faculty?

Senior administrators at Babson mentioned repeatedly the desire to "attract faculty" with Babson Interactive. The subsidiary gave administrators the option to pay more, grant equity in the company, and pay royalties to faculty. Moore stated that the equity issue "loomed large" as a means to "give star faculty equity opportunities if we needed to attract them." Moore noted that the board of trustees was worried that the College otherwise risked "losing its best talent."

Ronald Weiner, the owner of a New York City financial services firm, a Babson College trustee, and a member of the Babson Interactive board of directors, affirmed:

We felt that on a long-term basis we wanted to be able to attract and retain entrepreneurial talent. And to do so, we had to be competitive in the for-profit marketplace. We needed a for-profit structure with comparability of benefits, otherwise, we'd have inherent conflict between the compensation environment in the nonprofit world versus the compensation environment in the for-profit world.

Fetters commented further:

We wanted to say to faculty, 'You should want to work with us. You should not want to work with another distance learning company.' But we had to have some incentives, and the only way we could see to do that was to have a for-profit company where we could pay a royalty, or for really critical performers, give sort of a phantom stock option plan. We set up the for-profit to make people want to work with us, not to try to say you have to.

As a separate entity, NYUonline was positioned to appeal to the self-interest of faculty from across the university's thirteen schools. Finney stated:

"Because it was a freestanding company it was a way to use our faculty and have them profit from what they know, and their ability to communicate what they know. And that was a good side benefit." In addition to deterring faculty from contracting with other companies, Stedman also wanted to provide a vehicle to promote and further the interests of faculty who were eager to experiment with online teaching and learning.

> We were trying to encourage, empower and run with faculty interest, which was all over the place in this e-stuff, and create a modality to disinterest them from signing up with all these other places. We just wanted them to work with our own.

How do we retain key personnel?

The Fuqua School also worried about its inability to provide alternative compensation arrangements for faculty comparable to for-profit educational companies and other university competitors. Allan Lind, a Fuqua professor, noted:

> It was clear that we would lose some key personnel to our competitors—not school competitors but commercial competitors—if we didn't find a way to compensate them better than we could in the context of being Duke staff or faculty. We couldn't give them equity; there was nothing to give equity in. In addition, we were worried that our best internal faculty would stop doing our corporate executive education and go do it for Stanford, Northwestern or whoever else would pay better.

Rupp envisioned Fathom solving the same types of issues at Columbia:

> We founded Fathom . . . because we wanted to make sure we weren't just passive victims of other entities who got to the Internet first, and then picked off our key faculty and had them, for example, produce modules or segments for them. . . . We wanted to make sure that other for-profits especially, but maybe other universities, Harvard, for example, didn't wind up getting there ahead of us, having a site that was accessible all around the world, and then offering large payments to individual star faculty to be part of it.

Besides attracting faculty, the subsidiaries could limit the "brain drain" where faculty signed contracts to provide course content to other online education providers, whether for-profit companies or nonprofit universities. Rupp asserted that Columbia founded Fathom as an "offensive" strategy to "control our intellectual capital." Stedman, of NYU, remarked, "We were animated to create this thing in the first place because we wanted to have our cake and eat it too, so to speak."

> We didn't want our faculty to just take all this [content]—which is ours,
> our communities'—and just do whatever they wanted with it, with some
> ne'er do well, fast-paced, commercial, anti-intellectual, take us to the
> cleaners, for-profit thing. So we wanted to provide a way to say to the
> faculty, 'No, it's not about not doing it, we just want you to do it with
> us,' because then it would not be like consorting with some unknown
> foreign power; then it's all in the family.

Gerald Heeger, one of NYUonline's founders, concurred: "We created a for-
profit at NYU so that we [could] take advantage of the university's intellectual capital, but maintain control over that capital" (Lindquist, 1999,
February, p. 2).

SOLVING ORGANIZATIONAL PROBLEMS

How do we act quickly?

Colleges and universities are not known for streamlined processes, efficient
decision-making, or tidy lines of authority and accountability. Instead, adjectives like cumbersome, deliberate, and complicated are often used to describe
academic governance structures and processes (AGB, 1998; Benjamin et al.,
1993; Kennedy, 1994; Leatherman, 1998). Shared governance—which ideally
prescribes "joint action" (AAUP, 1990) among faculty, administrators and
trustees—can hinder efficient decision-making and management's ability to allocate resources and to set and implement priorities (Benjamin et al., 1993).
Faculty are the perceived villains. As Tierney states:

> There is something to be said for making a decision and moving on.
> Faculties are infamous for the opposite. They analyze an issue from
> every conceivable angle, study the topic a bit more, finally make a deci-
> sion at the last meeting of the school year, only to discover that a new
> committee the next year has decided to rethink what they have done.
> (Tierney, 1999, p. 149)

Advocates of shared governance view participation in the decisions and direction of the university as a fundamental value and characteristic of the
academy. A commitment to shared governance means "regular exchanges of
information and opinion, consultation, reflection, mediation, and compromise" (Scott, 2002, July-August). These actions protect the faculty's interests and ultimately ensure that the institution adheres to its mission (Gerber,
1997; Ramo, 1997). Shared governance presumably contributes to an atmosphere of trust among administrators, trustees, and faculty (Hanley,
2002, July-August). Any attempt to circumvent shared governance sacrifices

trust, goodwill, and "the concept of the university as a community" in the name of efficiency (Slaughter & Leslie, 1997).

The parent institutions recognized subsidiaries as a way to circumvent the perceived drawbacks of shared governance. Lloyd Short, NYUonline's senior vice president of e-learning, commented that the University's trustees decided early that online education "could more effectively be done outside the structure of the university" and that this may have been a larger motivation for creating the subsidiary than the company's need for capital or potential financial returns. Stedman believed that exclusion from NYU's governance structure provided "a greater opportunity for effective execution of the [company's] mission," and allowed NYUonline managers to create and implement business strategy without the "entanglements" of the University's governance system. "We wanted this to be controlled by us, but have a degree of independence so it had fluidity, speed, policy options, and a separation from the historic protocols of the place—so that it could make its own way."

The need for "independence," "speed," and "fluidity," in the marketplace provided a rationale for Babson Interactive. Fetters asserted that the subsidiary was created to avoid the "academic process for course approval," a process incongruent with the realities and time clock of the distance-learning environment. Moore contended, "If you remained part of Babson you would be caught up in the governance process of working with division chairs and getting approval by a curriculum committee." P. J. Guinan, a Babson professor and member of the board of directors of Babson Interactive, stated: "The theory was that to really make this work it needed to be an independent entity. That being a separate entity would give Tom more leverage, would sort of separate us from the school . . . to be more flexible." Allan Cohen, a Babson professor, concurred: "Tom knows how hard it is to move things through faculty. And he likes to be able to move faster than most faculty would like to move."

Detachment from NYU's governance structure also provided benefits to corporations eager to contract with NYUonline. David Hawthorne, senior vice president of e-learning environments at NYUonline, asserted:

> The last thing corporations wanted to deal with when it came to providing training and education for their employees, was universities. Corporations say, "They're bureaucratic, they're slow, they think they know more than we do, and they're arrogant. They don't want to do it our way and won't teach our culture, and that is what makes us different." So in that sense, structurally, a business or for-profit entity was essential. So we created a business friendly user interface by giving them a company that deals like a business, that has the look and feel of a

business, and that they can talk to like a business. And then on the other side of that interface, we face the university and we deal with all the bureaucracy and the sensitivities and the peccadilloes.

Kirschner declared that the idea of getting outside the "bureaucracy" of Columbia with Fathom was a fundamental motivation for the subsidiary. She asserted that Fathom was created as a for-profit company to be "a nimble, entrepreneurial organization," that would be able to compete more effectively in the extremely competitive arena of online services (Carr & Kiernan, 2000, p. A59). Sharyn O'Halloran, a Columbia professor, insisted that Fathom's founders,

> really felt that having an arm's length relationship [with the university] would give the entity the ability . . . to make strategic decisions, to actually forge ahead in a way that perhaps a not for-profit wouldn't be able to do. If it was a closer relationship with the university there would be a lot more politics involved, competing interests. It was a way of insulating it and allowing it to prosper.

Elizabeth Keefer, general counsel for Columbia, asserted that the entity had to reside outside Columbia's organizational structure in order to "have a more nimble vehicle" to conduct business. Ryan Craig, former vice president for business development at Fathom, noted that the company was developed as a legally separate for-profit entity to "avoid university bureaucracy and slowness, which characterizes university operations." Jonathan Cole, Columbia's provost, spoke of "trying to alter the nineteenth century models of the university" to better serve entrepreneurially-minded faculty.

Similarly, Wanda Wallace was outspoken about the necessity for Duke CE to separate from Fuqua:

> The reason for wanting to leave Duke University was to leave behind the bureaucracy—the hiring practices, the tenure practices—five different chains of command to get something done that takes six months. We wanted the flexibility and nimbleness to be able to move quickly in the market.

PROBLEMS UNSOLVED

Babson, Columbia, Duke, and NYU were beset by a number of problems—increased competition, the need for new sources of revenue and capital, threats from competitor institutions, the imperative to safeguard intellectual property, and the need for speedy decisions. The solution to all these problems was the for-profit subsidiary. In the garbage can of choice, decision-makers had fastened on one solution to multiple challenges.

This one solution, however, turned out not to be the answer. As of mid-2002, none of the subsidiaries had reached financial break-even. Though begun with great promise, Fathom had generated only $750,000 in revenue on costs of around $30 million, and in January 2003, was officially closed. After investing approximately $25 million, NYU ended NYUonline, due to lack of revenues and an uncertain market for online corporate education. Duke Corporate Education has struggled to meet financial projections, particularly since the September 11th tragedy. Babson Interactive has had no public operational or financial difficulties and hopes to soon show a profit from operations.

While prospects for outside capital was a prime motivator for for-profit subsidiaries, as of late 2002, none of the companies had received private capital investments. Instead, the parent institution funded the enterprise, either through investments of institutional reserves or by a guaranteed line of credit backed by the university's assets. The softening of the external capital market in the wake of the dot-com bust in late 2000 and early 2001 clearly affected these companies' fortunes. In the end, the universities decided to maintain complete control of the subsidiary, undiluted by surrendering seats on the company's board of directors to outside investors under unfavorable terms.

None of the subsidiaries separated entirely from the parent institution's governance system, though Duke Corporate Education and NYUonline (before it shut down) moved the furthest in this regard; Babson Interactive still remains very integrated. Right up until it was closed, Fathom was buffeted by inquiries from the University Senate regarding its finances and governance.

Finally, in several cases, the business background, perspective, and even language of the subsidiaries' managers has alienated faculty and hindered the joint effort essential to success. Managerial expertise in markets and products—driven by bottom-line discipline—has not in every case solved each company's personnel needs, but instead has often been a point of friction.

FINDING MESSAGES TO MATCH THE CULTURE

Though these subsidiaries were clearly established to solve specific problems, there was another layer of messages that posed a competing set of rationales for the subsidiaries. These asserted that the subsidiary was not about revenue generation, but about the need for capital in order to preserve university resources; not about circumventing shared governance, but about advancing the university's core mission and serving faculty; not about exploiting new markets, but about serving new constituencies; not about controlling intellectual property, but about providing new economic opportunities for faculty. In essence, the creation of the subsidiary was not about destroying values, but about protecting them. As the disjuncture between academic and corporate culture intensified, administrators were compelled to reassure their constituents that these companies would not compromise core values or destroy the academic culture.

Perhaps the clearest illustration of these competing rationales was at Duke University and the Fuqua School. Duke CE was created to solve financial, strategic and organizational problems; however, the subsidiary was also seen as the answer to cultural conflict in the Fuqua School (Bleak, 2001, June). The company was born in paradox—as a savior of academic culture, yet also as a giant step into the marketplace.

Duke CE was heralded not as a threat to the culture or bedrock values of the School, but as a means to preserve and perhaps insulate Fuqua's traditional academic research culture by separating the commercial aspects of executive education. Sheppard maintained that Duke CE was a boon, not a menace, to the university's academic culture: "This is not about changing the fabric of the university. It is about enhancing the university. The mission of education is to make people self-sufficient. We are providing an answer to global learning and life-long learning." Lange called Duke CE "an expression of Duke University."

Operationally, the separation from Fuqua allowed Duke CE to compensate faculty at levels not otherwise possible and to retain practice-oriented faculty. Duke CE's relationship to Fuqua was likened to the relationship of a hospital or clinic with a medical school—a place where the research and knowledge gained in the School could be applied in a cost-driven environment. The use of an acceptable academic analogy to describe the relationship between the organizations, rather than a pure business analogy, is consistent with the desire and need for the subsidiary to gain legitimacy and acceptance with the Fuqua academic community.

Unlike the other three subsidiaries, Duke CE was the only company whose creation was debated openly and formally approved by faculty. Because faculty approval was required and roles had to be clarified, the messages had to be carefully crafted for multiple constituents. Sheppard touted the alignment of the company with Duke's mission. Yet, he also acknowledged forthrightly that he was running a business to make money: "There is no question in anybody's mind that [Duke CE's] primary objective is to maximize the value of the shares. Everybody in this organization is clear on that. No question."

At Columbia, Kirschner articulated Fathom's operations as a means "to serve faculty and hold the academic community together in a very positive way." Rupp stated that Fathom was not founded "as an entrepreneurial money-making venture," but as a strategic means to further Columbia's mission in the Internet environment; however, he also stated that revenue generation would be a key goal. Kirschner noted that one of the motivations to become involved with Fathom was the opportunity "to extend a university online and provide points of access all over the world" (Carlson, 2000b, p. A45). Similarly, Ryan Craig asserted that Fathom would be a "literal projection of the university." Provost Jonathan Cole concurred:

> In terms of the transmission of knowledge and access to knowledge . . . it fits very much into the university's mission. . . . It potentially will bring knowledge and information to people who otherwise are not beneficiaries of the knowledge that's created out of the educational and cultural institutions that are part of Fathom.

Cole also spoke of a "revolution" in the way knowledge was produced in a university, but argued that even with this change, "it will be possible to safeguard the underlying values of the university" (Arenson, 2000, August 2). He commented further, "I think the dominant values are predominantly the same as they used to be. The income is only a means to pursue our mission. (p. A25)" Here the message was layered nicely, with the mission and values of the university at center stage and the potential financial windfall of the for-profit subsidiary positioned only as a means to further that mission. These comments sought to send the message, surely more in line with Columbia's culture, that the subsidiary was a means to an end: to advance the University's mission.

The duality (some would say hypocrisy) of the language at Columbia reflected the need for ambiguity in order to achieve consensus—the need, both politically and symbolically to cloak the case for the subsidiaries in the larger, loftier goals of the institutions. Clarity in purpose could have been the kiss of death for Fathom and in a similar way for NYUonline. In contrast, Duke CE's purpose was known and approved by faculty, allowing Sheppard to speak more clearly about the company's purposes.

Cohen and March (1986) include "ambiguity of purpose" (p. 195) as a fundamental characteristic of colleges and universities. They describe administrative leaders in universities as working "within a normative context that presumes purpose and within an organizational context that denies it" (p. 197). Leaders must avoid the level of specificity in administrative actions and decisions that will destroy acceptance and operate at a level of generality that will facilitate acceptance. The various messages conveyed by administrators regarding the subsidiaries confirm the anarchic nature of higher education institutions, where clear objectives do not often exist, "and the processes by which [these] objectives are established and legitimized are not extraordinarily sensitive to inconsistency" (p. 197). The messages are also themselves indicators of both the power of culture and the recognition of the need by administrators to "speak the language" of the constituency.

Leaders who operate with multiple messages have been labeled as Machiavellian and deceitful. Yet a certain "minor Machiavellianism" (Cohen & March, 1986, p. 205), has a high degree of utility in colleges and universities (Julius, Baldridge, & Pfeffer, 1999, March/April). Because the goals of universities are "extremely ambiguous," the list of legitimate activities can be "extremely long" (p. 114). Therefore, savvy advocates can usually make a plausible case for a program or action, clad in the history, mission, and priorities of the institution (Chaffee & Tierney, 1988; see also Kotter, 1996). Because organizational culture establishes the outer boundary for decisions, legitimacy accrues when a proposal echoes the institution's espoused values and basic assumptions. Therefore, leaders are pressed to both symbolically and substantively convey action within the context of organizational values (Birnbaum, 1988). In this sense, symbolism may be even more important than substance and a course of action guided by values more persuasive than an instrumental argument based on survival (Birnbaum, 1992).

Kanter (1983) asserts that leaders often have to undertake a careful "rewriting of corporate history" (p. 284) in order to make a change initiative or course of action palatable to constituencies. "To be effective, [university administrators] must align their strategies with their institution's culture rather than compete with it" (Birnbaum, 1992, p. 10). In fact, "one of the prime uses of the past is in the construction of a story that makes the future seem to grow naturally out of it in terms compatible with the organization's culture" (Kanter, 1983, p. 283). Framed in light of an institution's history and values, controversial administrative actions often begin to look more like "obvious choices" (p. 285), even to once skeptical constituencies.

Like Columbia, NYU argued that the for-profit subsidiary reinforced the mission of the university and reflected core values. For NYU, this came not so much in talking about the future of the institution, with NYUonline as a means for distributing knowledge, but in invoking NYU's past. Finney referred to this past as "a history of entrepreneurism and poverty." Stedman remarked that from its beginnings, NYU had been entrepreneurial in increasing its prestige and assuring financial viability. With this history as backdrop, he asserted that NYU's ambition to be among the elite research universities in the country necessitated the creation of NYUonline:

> NYU is a place that is transforming itself in the last generation or so. And has legitimately moved into the top tier of American universities. But we're not in the top of the top tier. And so it's timely. And in a certain kind of way, if not NYU, who?

However, Stedman contended that NYUonline was fully consistent with the history and values of NYU: "This was a logical next step for us, given what is going on in the world—Internet, computers, and all the capability that exists out there."

But the parallel most often drawn by Stedman, Finney, and others was with NYU's School of Continuing and Professional Studies (SCPS). With an annual enrollment of approximately 60,000 students, SCPS, the largest institution of its kind in the nation, is a force in continuing and distance education. The school serves a non-traditional student population; close to 80 percent of enrolled students work full-time and most are between the ages of 25 and 45. The school offers more than 2,000 credit and non-credit courses, many of these online through its "Virtual College." Hawthorne noted that NYUonline was "true to the mission of SCPS," and therefore, a good fit at NYU. Stedman asserted that because of SCPS, NYU had "a cultural acceptance" of NYUonline "in the body politic of the faculty." The lack of objection from faculty to NYUonline supports that assertion.

Administrators seemed secure in the fact that the creation of NYUonline was a natural extension of NYU's history. Yet, the basic assumption seemed to be that any action was acceptable if it ultimately elevated the prestige or wealth of the university. Again, the faculty's silence provided validation. This concurs with a body of research showing that universities are "prestige maximizers" (Slaughter & Leslie, 1997, p. 122), allocating resources in an attempt to increase institutional prestige, particularly in comparison with peer institutions (See Abbott, 1974, March; Breneman, 1970; Fairweather, 1988; Gross & Grambusch, 1968; Newman & Couturier, 2001, October).

At Babson, both administrators and faculty spoke of how it was essential for the College to create a for-profit subsidiary in order to be true to its mission and cultural assumptions. Bill Lawler, a tenured professor, stated that it was natural for Babson to create the company, because "this school practices what it preaches." Fetters asserted that the creation of the company presented no problems and that faculty fully supported the idea. "The business faculty by and large say, 'You know, we're a business faculty. You gotta do this stuff.'" Moore confirmed that the creation of the subsidiary substantiated the college's deepest values:

> It shows that we as a school are entrepreneurial, that we're getting in the market early on and we're demonstrating our competence in integrating educational materials in an innovative way. . . . If Babson is an entrepreneurial school, how can we not be in this space taking a leadership role?

Benson seconded that view: "This is about Babson as an entrepreneurial place. Babson as an innovative place. If we're going to maintain our image and our market position, this is an absolutely required expenditure." Fetters concluded that the founding of Babson Interactive was "just not that big a deal to us." Its founding was not controversial because basic assumptions at Babson College trumpeted entrepreneurial activity and the College's faculty was comfortable with the for-profit model. In essence, Babson's culture not only facilitated, but necessitated Babson Interactive.

Babson Interactive symbolically solidified the College's sense of self— "We are entrepreneurial"—and signaled to outside constituencies the institution's willingness to try new things and to practice what it preaches. Fetters declared, "We are known to be innovative. We're acting entrepreneurially, which is very consistent with our strategy. And we are known for that, so we have to practice it."

One could conjecture that if Babson had not created the subsidiary, its constituents would have questioned why the College had not entered the on-line education market when so many others had. Inaction at a time when entrepreneurial activity was proliferating all around them would have been incongruent with Babson's culture and could have potentially caused more problems than creating the subsidiary did.

Thus, the for-profit subsidiary became a "statement of values" (Chait, Holland, & Taylor, 1993, p. 24), and served "to exemplify and reinforce the organization's core values" (p. 9). When asked if creating Babson Interactive was in line with Babson's culture, Fetters responded:

> Yes. Well, we feel that we're incredibly entrepreneurial. Not only do we teach entrepreneurship and have a lot of students who come here because they're going to start their own businesses and they're going to be entrepreneurial majors, or they just want to be around entrepreneurs, . . . but we also think that we operate entrepreneurially.

In hopes of indicating cultural alignment, every institution mentioned the congruity of the for-profit subsidiary with the parent institution's mission, with Columbia and NYU administrators the most vocal. Interestingly, this talk clearly demonstrated the desire for the founders and managers of the companies to appeal to faculty values and display alignment with academic culture. Babson's leaders mentioned this only in passing. Perhaps this was because at Babson, it was a given, so embedded in culture it did not need to be reinforced.

The decisions of university administrators and subsequent actions "send important signals about what the institution values" (Steiner, 2000, August 7, p. A22). At Columbia and NYU, the creation of the for-profit subsidiary sent a signal that was not altogether congruent with the existing culture of the parent institution. Therefore, that signal had to be modified by other messages extolling the alignment of the company with the parent institution's mission and culture. At Babson College, the signal was business as usual; no alarms were set off when Babson Interactive was created. At Fuqua, faculty approved the subsidiary's creation, granting legitimacy to its business purposes.

These multiple messages go to the heart of the for-profit subsidiary in the nonprofit university. In essence, they show that goals can (or must) be framed in different terms for different audiences—more like translation than deceit—and can be interpreted as signals and echoes of the values and beliefs guiding and supporting the cultures of the two organizational types. They show the potential for conflict between an organizational structure centered on the values of profit generation and value maximization, and a parent organization focused on knowledge generation and prestige maximization.

SUMMING UP

Several conclusions can be drawn from the creation of these subsidiaries.

- The for-profit subsidiaries were created as the single solution to a set of complex financial, competitive, and organizational problems experienced by each parent institution.
- The decision-making process that generated this single solution was consistent with the conception of the university as an organized anarchy. In the end, however, the problems largely remained unsolved.
- Though administrators and managers associated with Fathom and NYUonline argued that the subsidiary would solve the stated problems, they also sought to align the purpose of the for-profit subsidiary with the parent institution's mission, values, and history. Often, this dual set of messages seemed contradictory, making it hard to determine the subsidiary's real purpose. Clarity of purpose would have been disastrous for

Fathom and NYUonline, whereas ambiguity helped provide legitimacy within the broad goals of the university.

- The degree of congruence with the culture of the parent institution was revealed in the quantity and nature of the messages offered by administrators of the parent and managers of the subsidiary about the reason for the company's creation. The more congruence between the subsidiary's and parent's culture, the less these messages contradicted themselves. This congruity was seen at Babson Interactive and to a lesser degree at Duke Corporate Education.

Chapter Three
Governance: Who's in Charge?

A Fathom executive lamented the several layers of approval she had to navigate in order to send an email touting Fathom's wares to Columbia's alumni; nonetheless, she did it and later acknowledged the need to respect Columbia's processes. NYUonline's chief executive spoke passionately and often of the value of an advisory board, composed of NYU's deans and distinguished faculty, yet never created one before the company's demise. Several Duke Corporate Education managers expressed the need to de-emphasize the natural deference and positional authority accorded faculty and create a flat organization, yet Duke CE formed a group of "Academic Directors"—all current or former professors—with a visible governance role. Babson Interactive asserted the necessity of being outside Babson's governance mechanism, yet created two faculty oversight committees with direct links to the College's faculty governance body.

At the root of these seemingly contradictory actions is culture. These incidents illustrate culture's influence on the governance of the for-profit subsidiaries of nonprofit universities and highlight the dual nature of these companies.

In business the acquisition of a company or the merger of two companies has become a stage for the drama of cultural conflict (Schein, 1999). Mergers and acquisitions, though seen by many business leaders as the rational combination of two company's processes, technologies, and personnel to achieve greater efficiencies and competitive advantage, are often fraught with difficulties; the tombs of failed mergers and acquisitions pock the corporate landscape. The cultural hazards of combining two organizational realities contributed to the high failure rate. Schein (1999) observes that in the case of acquisitions and mergers, "surprisingly little attention is paid to culture" (p. 8).

Though the creation of for-profit subsidiaries by non-profit universities is neither an acquisition nor a merger, it is comparable because of the attempt to blend two disparate cultures. In any marriage, there is both harmony and friction, and this is especially true in the governance of for-profit subsidiaries of nonprofit universities.

This chapter is on governance. In the case of these subsidiaries, it answers the governance questions: "Who is in charge; who makes decisions; who has a voice; and how loud is that voice" (Rosovsky, 1990, p. 261)?

CULTURE AND GOVERNANCE

Culture controls. It is a powerful regulating and governing force in organizations, effectively guiding and instructing organizational participants as to "the way things are done around here." Culture gives meaning and predictability to work life (Schein, 1999, p. 25), providing a stability that organizational participants come to rely on and help maintain. Because culture is at the center of how work is done and how decisions are made, it shapes governance structures and processes (Masland, 1991).

A precise definition of governance is almost as elusive as a definition of culture. Birnbaum (1988) contended that governance is the answer to the question, "Who's in charge here?" (p. 4). Similarly, Chait (2002) defined governance as "the distribution of legitimate authority for the purposes of making decisions and taking actions" (p. 69). Because governance concerns human relationships, social processes, and the underlying assumptions that function in decision-making and action, culture and governance are inextricably intertwined (Masland, 1991; Schein, 1992).

Culture provides a template for acceptable organizational policies, procedures, and structures, and a groundwork for governance. Once established, successful governance processes and structures then reinforce and validate cultural assumptions about governance (Hollinger, 2001, May-June; Schein, 1992). Culture and governance interact. Guided by culture's influence, organizational participants are socialized to act in a way that has been proven to solve organizational problems, these actions become policy and process and guide future behaviors, and these behaviors, when viewed as effective, are then institutionalized as culture (Arnold & Capella, 1985; Deal & Kennedy, 1982; Schein, 1992). Culture then defines for organizational participants "what to pay attention to, what things mean, how to react emotionally to what is going on, and what actions to take in various kinds of situations" (Schein, 1992, p. 22). When culture is threatened, organizational participant's view of reality and appropriate responses are threatened or altered too (Kotter & Heskett, 1992). In these circumstances, organizational participants become defensive and seek to protect their way of life by working to restore their shared "social reality" (Birnbaum, 1988,

p. 72). Culture thus defines the boundaries for acceptable governance processes and structures and imposes sanctions when these boundaries are violated.

DECISION-MAKING IN THE ACADEMY AND THE CORPORATION

Governance is exercised "for the purpose of making decisions" (Chait, 2002, p. 69). Indeed, decision-making is at the very heart of governance. Yet, it is here that the academy and corporation perhaps differ most markedly.

Characterized by diffuse authority and decentralized decision-making, academic governance is typically "shared" by faculty, administrators, and trustees and is considered one of the "core values" of the academy (Ruch, 2001, p. 141). (See also Gerber, 2001, May-June; Glotzbach, 2001, May-June; Hamilton, 2001, Spring; Kezar, 2001; Rhodes, 2000, September). In academic governance, inactivity prevails, participation is fluid, and interest group behavior and conflict often dominate discourse among governing bodies (Baldridge, Curtis, Ecker, & Riley, 1977; Cohen & March, 1974). Often mere persistence is the key to influence in a university (Birnbaum, 1988; Cohen & March, 1974). These characteristics, particularly prominent in prestigious research universities and liberal arts colleges (Baldridge, 1971a; Baldridge, Curtis, Ecker, & Riley, 1978; Gerber, 1997), produce a governance system that is at times "cumbersome" (AGB, 1998, p. 4; see also Whitaker, 2001) where decisions are "rarely made by either bureaucratic fiat or simple consensus" (Baldridge, 1971a, p. 8).

The ideals of shared governance were articulated by the American Association of University Professors' 1966 *Statement on Government of Colleges and Universities* (AAUP, 1990), which has been considered the standard for the practice of academic governance and "the foundation of the shared governance movement" (Cox, 2000, p. 1). The Statement extols "interdependence" and "joint action" (p. 1) in governance, while outlining the roles of the board, the president, and the faculty. (See also Mortimer & McConnell, 1978.) Highlighting the "inescapable interdependence" (p. 2) these groups share, the Statement gives considerable discretion to the faculty, while circumscribing the authority of the president and board in decision-making. Speaking of different decision-making circumstances, the Statement reads:

> In some instances, an initial exploration or recommendation will be made by the president with consideration by the faculty at a later stage; in other instances, a first and essentially definitive recommendation will be made by the faculty, subject to the endorsement of the president and the governing board. In still others, a substantive contribution can be made when student leaders are responsibly involved in the process. (p. 3)

The Statement advises that each of the governing constituencies "have a voice" in determining budgets, priorities, strategic plans, and future expenditures (p. 3). This Statement has been incorporated, in letter or in spirit, into the policies and processes of many colleges and universities.

The demand for voice and consultation in academic decision-making has no counterpart in the corporation, where decision-making and authority tend to be centralized. Driven by the overarching goals of profitability and shareholder value, corporate governance "involves the exercise of authority or power toward a particular end" (Lorsch & MacIver, 1989, p. 12). (See also Besse, 1973; Blair, 1995; Monks & Minow, 1995; Oster, 1995.) With the profit motive dominant, "a corporation . . . is always an authoritarian organization" (Besse, 1973, p. 108), seeking efficiencies everywhere. This quest for efficiency has traditionally yielded a "command and control" governance model (Sifonis & Goldberg, 1996, p. 96), characterized by top-down authority, hierarchical organizational structures, and centralized power, all driven by the "bottom-line" (Giroux, 1999; Pound, 2000; Sifonis & Goldberg, 1996). Consonant with these values, decision-making in the for-profit company "emphasizes speed in exploiting competitive advantages and secrecy in developing those advantages" (Oster, 1995, p. 13). Because decision by formal authority is highly efficient, it is the preferred decision-making mode in corporations (Schein, 1988).

Both inside and outside the academy, there have been calls to adopt the same approach in universities (AGB, 1998; Benjamin et al., 1993; Carlin, 1999; Leatherman, 1998; Sowell, 1998, September 7). Advocates assert that shared governance is inadequate for the modern university and inappropriate to respond quickly to competitive pressures and to constituents' demands for accountability (Benjamin et al., 1993; Cole, 1994; Kennedy, 1994). Proponents of a more corporate style of governance, advocate granting greater power to the university president, centralizing decision structures, and streamlining decision processes to more efficiently meet the demands of the modern academic environment (AGB, 1996; Duderstadt, 2000a, 2000b).

In response to these calls for reform, advocates of shared governance contend that "intellectual life . . . is different from business life" (Scott, 2002, July-August, p. 43) and that important benefits to the academic community and perhaps even the fundamental mission of higher education will be lost (Baldwin & Leslie, 2001, Spring; Collie & Chronister, 2001, Spring; Kezar, 2001). Collegiality will diminish, distrust and skepticism will increase and the culture and tradition of the academy will be irreparably damaged. Participation in governance, for many faculty, "is what separates the academic life as a profession from the academic life as simply a career or job" (Hanley, 2002, July-August, p. 2). The expertise and professional status of faculty demand inclusion in governance (Ramo, 1997). Because the professional status of the professoriate is linked to the state of shared governance (Baldridge, 1971b; Etzioni, 1991), the loss of shared governance is considered a blow to the faculty's professional status (Hanley, 2002, July-August; Ramo, 1997; Rhodes, 2000, September). Regular exchanges of information, consultation, and joint decision-making protect the faculty's interests and preserve an institution's mission (Gerber, 2001, May-June; Scott, 2002, July-August). More importantly, though, "the faculty's role in governance is the foundation of academic freedom" (Scott, 2002, July-August, p. 42). Because of the importance of shared governance to the academic "community" (Baldridge, 1971a; Gerber, 1997; Millett, 1962), any attempt to circumvent shared governance in the name of corporate efficiency, is considered a sacrifice of trust, goodwill, and "the concept of the university as a community" (Slaughter & Leslie, 1997). (See also Birnbaum, 2000; Gumport, 2001, Spring; Rhodes, 2000, September.) For-profit subsidiaries were considered a chief offender in the onslaught against shared governance.

CEO's Role in Decision-making

The CEO of each subsidiary had substantial discretion in decision-making, at least internally. When decisions had the potential to affect the parent institutions however, the CEO's discretion was constrained.

Babson Interactive CEO Tom Moore was the driving force behind the company's decisions. Allan Cohen, a Babson professor, commented, "Moore definitely has the most decision-making power at Babson Interactive; there's no question." Michael Fetters, Babson College's vice president for academics, also names Moore as the most influential voice in the company's decision processes. Internally, Moore had ultimate authority over salaries, personnel decisions, and the company's budget. Leo Higdon, Babson's president at the time the subsidiary was founded, gave Moore discretion to use $2.5 million from the College.

Similarly, at Duke CE, Blair Sheppard was clearly the company's guiding force. Once the budget was established and approved by Duke CE's board of directors, Sheppard bore ultimate responsibility for all internal matters. Within the confines set by the board, "we're free to do whatever we want to do," Sheppard remarked.

Like Sheppard and Moore, Ann Kirschner was ultimately responsible for all operational decisions at Fathom, as well as all personnel and budgetary allocations. "Nobody's looking over my shoulder," she commented. After the budget was approved by Fathom's board, Kirschner, as one of her vice presidents put it, "runs the show." However, Michael Crow's role in the company was significant. As Columbia's executive vice provost and a member of Fathom's board of directors, Crow described his role in decision-making at Fathom at three levels. For operational decisions, Kirschner had supremacy; for "tactical" decisions, as Crow explained, he and Kirschner consulted; and on "strategic" issues, Crow consulted with the board and then Kirschner implemented the decision.

The thread tying these three types of decisions together was Crow. Rollow asserted that Crow did not make direct operational decisions, but he oversaw budget allocation decisions and would "ask questions" about other operational decisions. In operational decisions, his presence was felt, even if indirectly.

More than any of the other three subsidiaries, NYUonline's CEO, Gordon Macomber, was at the top of the company's internal hierarchy. Upon joining the company, he assembled his own management team and changed the company's business strategy. He was the ultimate decision-maker on budgetary, strategic, and personnel issues, though he involved other company executives. When a key decision had to be made, Macomber made it.

The process by which these decisions were made reflected the managerial background of Macomber as well as the other top staff. All former corporate executives, NYUonline's managers had ingrained a corporate model of governance and changed the tenor of decision-making from when the company was operated by academic administrators. According to Robert Manual, an NYU administrator who helped manage NYUonline in its first year of operation, "all major decisions" were made "in consultation with William Berkley [chair of the NYUonline board], Stedman, and Jay Oliva [NYU's president]." Conversely, Jeff Tagliabue, NYUonline's director of finance, commented on the company's current state of decision-making, "We've got a good deal of autonomy. We make all decisions—hiring, salary, space—most everything. We are on our own; we do everything." David Finney, dean of NYU's School of Professional and Continuing Studies and a member of the NYUonline board of directors, concurred:

> In terms of the actual business strategy and the pursuit of that, . . . the board has tried to not put any fences around it. It's Gordon and his people. He has to have room to get a group of people deeply invested in a concept, and make it happen. And I think the university has been committed to allowing him to do that.

These four chief executives held significant power in decision-making within their companies, similar to a corporate CEO, but in sharp contrast to the traditional power of a university president. Cohen and March (1986) note that "the president's role [in decision-making is] more commonly sporadic and symbolic than significant. . . . The president has modest control over the events of college life" (p. 2), about as much as the driver of a car skidding on ice. Birnbaum (1988) concurs, presidents "may not be able to make dramatic changes in their institutions most of the time" (p. 203). Clearly the subsidiary CEO had internal authority more in line with a corporate executive than an academic president.

Decision-making Processes

A key rationale for creating for-profit subsidiaries as separate organizations was to be free from the parent's governance structures and processes in order to act with speed and flexibility. However, none of the subsidiaries was able to separate totally from its parent's governance processes, though the degree of separation varied considerably among the four companies. The normative influence of consensual decision-making and collaboration, hallmarks of academic governance, was strong, influencing each company's leaders to employ variations of these decision-making processes. This was quite visible at Duke CE and Fathom.

The original business plan for Duke CE called for "swift" curricular design and speed in response to customer demands. Even the process of creating the company (10 weeks) was remarkably fast compared to the normal decision processes of the Fuqua School, where a decision of such magnitude could take a year or more. Sheppard asserted that a distinctive characteristic of Duke CE has been an ability to respond quickly to client's needs and market demand. Bob Reinheimer, a Fuqua professor now at Duke CE, proclaimed that decisions were frequently "made on the spot." One of the reasons for the quick decision time, Reinheimer stated, was that there were "no faculty areas that have to bless things."

Even with the accelerated speed in decision-making, there were still hints of academic decision-making at Duke CE. For decisions that had business ramifications for the entire company, Reinheimer asserted that the preferred mode was for the key decision-maker to poll as many people as possible within the company before the decision was made. Reinheimer stated that after this process was complete, when he "has a good enough score, [the decision-maker] says 'Yes' or 'No.'" This process evokes the academic preference for collaborative and consensual decision-making. Sim Sitkin, a Fuqua professor on leave for two years to Duke CE, related his efforts to instill a more "collegial type" of decision-making in the company.

When key decisions were to be made, and the decision did not have to be made quickly, Sitkin would send emails to all interested parties in order to gain their input. When that input was gathered, he would then make a recommendation to the executive committee and Sheppard, who would render a final decision. The desire for consultation reflected the backgrounds of the decision-makers.

Academic governance spawns a plethora of committees; indeed, academic decisions are typically made by committees. In this regard, Duke CE employed governance structures that recalled the company's academic roots. Sitkin commented that there were "lots and lots of committees" in the company. Both standing and ad hoc committees—put together quickly to solve a problem—were most often "cross-functional" in composition, in order to more effectively handle operational issues that span the range of company functions.

Reinheimer, however, characterized these committees as operational teams—a more business-like term. These teams were project-based, constructed largely to serve a client's needs. The use of teams, according to Sheppard, resulted from devolution of authority in the company since its inception, when it was basically governed by an executive committee and an academic council.

Within Duke CE, the management reporting structure ended with Sheppard. He had ultimate decision-making authority, yet rarely made decisions in isolation. Sheppard worked collaboratively with the two other top managers in the company, John Gallagher and Judy Rosenblum. The company's team-based work style and flat management structure leveled the playing field among decision-makers. In many ways, the company's management style could be termed "collegial" and revolved around soliciting, when possible, a wide range of input. When a decision was required quickly, Sheppard would make the decision, with input from Gallagher and Rosenblum. At the operational level, however, the team-based structure prevailed. Reinheimer stated: "The team runs the show. Yes, Blair attempts to stick his nose into things, but we throw him out. And he's gotten quite good about just giving up and going away."

The company's emphasis on team-based work is consistent with recent business practices. However, in the academic governance literature, teams have also been considered an appropriate structure for university governance and management (Bensimon & Neumann, 1993). Birnbaum (1992) asserts, "The value of teams is clearly consistent with academic norms of collegiality and shared governance" (p. 39). This way of working at Duke CE showed a commitment to collegiality and exhibits a desire for broad communication among company personnel. Yet, an important difference with academic governance remained. Whereas consultation and broad input in decisions are demanded in traditional academic governance, Sheppard ultimately held the authority to decide whether to solicit input in decisions or to just make them individually. The subsidiary's employees understood that decisions could legitimately be made without consultation through the team-based structure.

At Fathom, David Wolff, vice president for educational programming, remarked that the subsidiary's for-profit structure enabled faster decisions than was typical for a nonprofit organization. Despite this assertion, however, Fathom was constrained by the decision-making style of its parent and the other consortium members, even though, according to Wolff, the company "looked like any other for-profit." Rollow noted that because of Fathom's tie to thirteen other academic and nonprofit members of its consortium, company managers were "careful of the process" when making decisions that involved faculty at Columbia or the other member institutions and that Fathom "respected their operational processes."

For example, when Fathom partnered with the American Association of Retired Persons (AARP) to provide educational content on the AARP's website, the subsidiary realized paid advertisements would be inappropriate next to a professor's educational material. Therefore, Rollow sought the approval of each consortium member in order to ensure that only appropriate material would be displayed. This assurance from Rollow was crucial to the deal. She described the care Fathom took in working with members of the consortium as part of a "very different mindset than I think the average commercial property might have."

This mindset was also evident in the process Fathom followed with Columbia's alumni office when negotiating to send a promotional email to alumni. Ultimately, Rollow had to negotiate "four layers of approval" before the email was sent, but later said this was necessary in order to maintain "partner relations" and to show "trust and an understanding of shared values."

The reasons for attention to process were contested however. Though Rollow stressed that a concern for shared values was at its root, Ryan Craig, a former Fathom vice president who left the company in 2000 to join a venture capital firm, noted that it was an issue of ownership. "We have to listen," asserted Craig. "Because the universities control Fathom. . . . We have to listen." To Craig, Fathom's deference to process was not about trust or respect, but about ownership and its incumbent accountability.

Babson Interactive's decision process was closely tied to its parent. Internally, Moore made the company's operational and budgetary decisions, conferring, as necessary, with Stephen Laster, the company's chief technology officer, and other managers. However, because of the company's small size—four full-time and two half-time employees—decisions were quite consensual.

Nevertheless, in making decisions, Moore consulted widely with the company's managers and with College administrators. For example, when making crucial decisions about the delivery of an MBA program for the Intel corporation, Fetters commented that Moore would

> bring everybody together that's going to be involved in the project and say, "Okay, let's get all the issues out on the table. Let's lay them all out and see where you all think we should be. And then Mike [Fetters] and I and the president [Higdon] will talk about this with the chairman of the board [Craig Benson] and make a decision."

Regardless of his decision-making power, Moore employed a very consultative process. Fetters continued, "My sense is that everything Tom Moore does he checks with [Babson President] Leo [Higdon], and then Leo checks with [Trustee] Craig Benson." This consultation did not end with Higdon or Benson, however. Moore admitted that he often conferred with Fetters on important issues, a style that Moore employed as dean and continued to use as CEO.

Decisions at NYUonline followed the organizational chart and culminated with Macomber, who changed the decision environment in the company from consultative and collegial to centralized and corporate when he and the other top managers joined NYUonline. The shift in NYUonline's decision-making was illustrated by the subsidiary's relationship with a software firm, which had helped build the technology platform for NYUonline's first courses. After working with the company and its products, Macomber and the other executives were dissatisfied with the quality of work. At that point, Macomber decided to end the relationship and instead build NYUonline's internal capabilities. The board was informed but not consulted.

NYUonline's managers had complete discretion. The overall attitude, summed up by one executive when speaking of the University's role in the venture, was "Fund it and get out of the way."

Decision-making Principles

In a university, decision-making is often diffuse and decentralized, and due to goal ambiguity, one would be hard pressed to identify guiding principles (Baldridge et al., 1977; Birnbaum, 1988; Cohen & March, 1974; Julius et al., 1999, March/April). Some would say serving students should animate decision-making; others argue that decisions should be driven by faculty interests; and others might make the case for the needs of the larger public. However, there is no paramount principle, like profitability, which guides and motivates decisions in the academy (AGB, 1998; Gerber, 1997; Ruch, 2001). Though the for-profit subsidiaries were not exclusively profit-driven, the principles guiding their decisions reflected business rather than academic concerns. However, the subsidiaries also exhibited the propensity to eschew the goal of profitability in order to follow alternate goals. This was particularly true for Babson Interactive and Fathom.

At Babson Interactive, the market played a significant role in decision-making. According to Moore, for non-degree courses, "the customer [is] the arbiter of quality." Fetters concurred:

> You just do what the client wants. . . . [The faculty] know that we have to move with the market, that the market is the arbitrator of what sells and what doesn't sell, and that if the market is demanding integrated education, we have to deliver that. If they are demanding online education, that's what we have to deliver.

Contrary to academic norms, where faculty often have the right to choose the courses they teach, Babson Interactive followed a market-driven philosophy. In fact, when asked how the company would respond to a proposal from a faculty member who thought he had an interesting idea for an online course, Moore responded, "We'd certainly listen, but this is market-driven, so the fact that a faculty member thought it was interesting would have very little bearing."

Even with these market-driven values, at least in the company's early stages, the motivation to meet a profit goal was a peripheral concern at best. Interestingly, no one mentioned profit as a guiding motive for the company or even as a metric for success. Moore quoted Craig Benson, chairman of the Babson Interactive board and a member of the College's board of trustees:

> I don't want any discussion about break even here. Babson ought to be throwing three million dollars away on experimentation, with the only outcome being they're smarter at the end of the year than they were at the beginning. . . . This is not about break even.

For Benson, it seemed that neither showing a profit nor even recouping the costs of doing business were crucial outcomes for the company.

Reinheimer described Duke CE's guiding decision-making principle as "client satisfaction uber alles." Its secondary consideration was the effect of the decision on Duke CE's financial health. Sheppard agreed that client satisfaction and profitability were the company's top priorities in decision-making:

> Our job is to be an excellent organization that services clients' needs in
> a way in which Duke would be proud. And because it's necessary, to
> maximize the value of the business. There is no question in anybody's
> mind that the primary objective is to maximize the value of the business.

He argued that the company was "client centered, . . . client focused, . . . and we make money." Nan Keohane, Duke University's president, stated that the company's main considerations were "providing excellent executive education and making money doing so." She added that "providing profitable executive education" was a key priority for the company.

At NYUonline decisions were made almost exclusively by the company's managers, rather than in collaboration with university administrators, as was the case in the company's first year. These decisions were clearly driven by "the corporate education market." From the outset, when the management team altered NYUonline's business plan from delivering courses to students—the "retail market"—to selling training materials and educational content to corporations, which was believed to be the larger and more lucrative market, the consumer-driven nature of the company's actions was readily apparent.

NYUonline's decisions were focused on capturing market share, building its clientele, and satisfying customers. At the root of these principles was the desire to grow the business and show positive financial returns.

At Fathom, though the business was created to bring a positive financial return, the guiding principles were more complex than profitability. Craig articulated the company's objectives as (1) "to build a sustainable, profitable business," and (2) "to serve the objectives of the University." Rupp, Columbia's president, argued that Fathom must "support the University," and Cole asserted that the subsidiary must "keep in mind the larger interests of the University writ large." Even in the midst of a rapidly shifting business environment that had caused other Internet ventures to alter their business models and strategies, Fathom clung to its intended purpose, even when financial returns did not quickly materialize, rather than change course abruptly and pursue what might be a more profitable strategy. This seemed to be a point of pride for one Fathom executive:

> We're not the same as some young start-ups, when the market first
> shifted, who said, "Oh, direct to consumer is out. Did I say I was direct
> to consumer? I really meant I was B to B [business to business]. Oh, did

I say B to B? I really meant I was wireless." We never went down that path. Instead we tried to figure out how to do direct to consumer smarter. . . . So I think we pat ourselves on the back a fair amount for . . . being able to ride the market wave.

As Rollow mentioned, Fathom was "as much mission driven as commercially driven."

Decision-making Constraints

Even with the authority the chief executives held within their companies, all four subsidiaries were constrained with respect to the legal contracts and business relationships they could consummate. These constraints were meant to protect the parent institution from embarrassment and even scandal over actions the subsidiary might take.

NYU required that its legal counsel review and approve all external contracts, even though NYUonline also retained a legal team. Tagliabue at first viewed this requirement as "cumbersome," but eventually just informed clients that, in order to avoid misunderstandings, contracts had to be reviewed by NYU. However, concern over the company's affiliations seemed to run even deeper. Macomber was required to update Berkley regularly on "what we are doing and who we are dealing with in contracts." Berkley then took this information to the executive and finance committees of NYU board of trustees, in order to keep them abreast of NYUonline's activities. Thus, through Berkley and the NYUonline board, the University's trustees maintained close oversight of the company's activities.

Likewise, policy established by the Duke CE board of directors, at the behest of the University's trustees, constrained Duke CE from executing contracts or partnerships with certain types of businesses. The company cannot serve clients in the sex or pornography industry, the tobacco industry, or that may be involved in illegal activities or practices. These measures were meant to keep the Duke name untainted and free from association with industries or companies employing questionable practices. The Duke CE board regularly monitors the company's list of current and potential clients.

Fathom's board also closely watched the quality of its partnerships in order to safeguard the University's name. Fathom's marketing was also circumscribed informally. Too much marketing or advertisements placed in the wrong position might be deemed improper and unseemly to the Columbia faculty and Fathom's consortium partners. This assurance was crucial to the completion of the deal with the AARP. Rollow commented: "So we don't just have carte blanche once we've been created as a company to then say,

'Oh, we're a for-profit company, we'll just syndicate the content on [our partner's] behalf.' It doesn't quite work that way." Fathom's management considered these constraints the proper way to effectively do business with the University in general, and its faculty in particular. In essence, paying close attention to Columbia's way of doing things—its culture—was a necessary cost of doing business for Fathom.

These constraints not only affected Kirschner and the rest of Fathom's management, but also Crow. Speaking of Crow, Rollow commented that because of Fathom's connection to Columbia, "he can't just do whatever he wants to do," but must act according to the guiding context and values of the University.

Similarly, Babson College's board required that a college administrator review every contract Babson Interactive entered and that Moore approve with the board of trustees any action, which if performed by Babson's president, would also require board approval. These requirements were meant to protect the reputation and interests of the College.

These are all significant constraints for companies in pursuit of profit. Ultimately, by restricting the range of clients these companies can serve or the business partnerships they could form, the boards and parent institutions limited each company's potential profitability. Thus, each subsidiary's potential for profitability was perhaps compromised by the need to remain true to the parent institution's guiding values and basic assumptions.

ACCOUNTABILITY AND REPORTING RELATIONSHIPS

In contrast to decision-making streams in universities—where problems and solutions intersect randomly and collide somewhat indiscriminately in decisional "garbage cans" (Cohen & March, 1974)—stands the corporate organizational chart consisting of straight lines, tidy boxes, and clear connections. These clear lines of authority and channels for communication suggest, at least on paper, tight-coupling among the organization's structures, participants, and operational processes. The corporate sector seeks to establish and communicate who is accountable to whom, for what, and why.

"Corporate governance has always been a matter of enforcing accountability" (Demb & Neubauer, 1992, p. 14). Accountability is not only achieved through a clear chain of command, but also through clearly defined, quantifiable measures of effectiveness: return on investment, profit per dollar of sales, or earnings per share, to name just a few (Besse, 1973). These measures are monitored continuously by management and regularly by the board of directors.

A university has no similar mechanisms for accountability, particularly in the academic realm (Besse, 1973; W. G. Bowen, 1994). "Unlike the corporation, there is nothing neat and orderly about the [university], nothing straightforward, nothing unambiguous, not much clearly defined" (Downey, 2000, p. 307). Accountability, if ever achieved, occurs through power sharing in a system of "checks and balances." Traditionally colleges and universities have functioned under a bicameral system, with an academic senate composed of faculty and a board of lay trustees. Though the board has final, legal responsibility for the organization, the institution's administration, with day-to-day control over operations and budgets, constitute a third "branch." In the best of times, accountability in a university is a complicated and complex proposition, where neither authority nor responsibility is clearly delineated.

Accountability in the for-profit subsidiaries was clear and ordered internally, yet often muddled and conflicted externally. In each company's board of directors, different arrangements illustrated the parent institution's level of comfort with the subsidiary and its managers. Each subsidiary's CEO answered in some degree to the company's board of directors, yet reporting channels multiplied after that, hinting at the influence of academic culture.

At Babson Interactive, Moore was legally accountable to the company's board of directors, yet in reality, he reported to Higdon, the College's president, rather than Benson, the company's chairman. This highlights the lack of clarity in accountability. Though Higdon was on the board of directors, he was content to take a backseat in the governance of the company, largely deferring to Benson. Fetters commented on Higdon's relationship to Benson: "Higdon relies heavily on Craig, because he knows that Craig can handle the board of trustees. He knows that if he does what Craig says, he's not going to get in trouble with the board." This relationship, while seeming to benefit Higdon by insulating him from board criticism, was not optimal for Moore. Fetters stated: "My sense is that Tom may like a little more guidance from Leo. It would be nice to have him be a little more of a decision-maker and push back on things."

Benson, however, is a key player in the company, not only by acting as a champion for Babson Interactive's interests with the board of trustees, but also by demanding a type of accountability not typical of academic governance. According to Fetters:

> Benson acts just like a venture capitalist. Craig wants to know what's happening all the time. If Tom makes predictions, he'd better hit those predictions. Craig wants Tom to move faster and faster, make more decisions.

. . . So I think Tom feels, and rightly so, that Craig's looking over his shoulder at all times.

As chair of Babson Interactive's board of directors, Benson reported to the executive committee of the College's board of trustees. Beneath Moore in the hierarchy of the company, the lines of accountability were clear. Fetters defined Moore's role in the company: "Basically what has been set up in the company is that Tom is pretty much an entrepreneur, so he gets to run the show. Then if he has questions he consults with [Higdon] or [Benson]."

Reporting relationships at Duke CE seemed straightforward at first glance, but on closer inspection revealed some ambiguity. Blair Sheppard reported directly to the company's board of directors, chaired by Douglas Breeden, dean of the Fuqua School. As dean, Breeden answered to Peter Lange, Duke's provost. Lange reported to Duke's president, Nan Keohane, who was accountable to the University's board of trustees. However, it was unclear to whom Breeden reported as chair of the Duke CE board of directors. Though Breeden reported to Lange in his role as academic dean, Lange was a member of the board Breeden chaired, thus confusing accountability. Neither Keohane nor a member of the University's board of trustees sat on the company's board. Keohane referred to this arrangement as "murky;" however, it has caused no problems so far.

Because of the lack of contact with the Duke board of trustees, Sheppard has made it a point to provide regular updates to the board's executive committee. Informally, Lange and Tallman Trask, Duke's executive vice president for administration, kept Keohane abreast of the company's condition and activity. In addition, Breeden updated the Fuqua faculty on the status of the company on a regular basis and also communicated with the School's board of visitors at its twice-yearly meetings.

At NYUonline, Macomber was directly accountable to the company's board, and in particular to Berkley, its chairman. "A good board is a well-advised board," Macomber stated and so he worked to keep the board well apprised. Tagliabue believed that the constant updating paid off with both NYUonline's board and the University's administration:

> I think they have a comfort level that they are not going to wake up two months from now and wonder what we are doing. We are really updating them on all ends—I am doing it on the legal side, Gordon is doing it both with the Provost and the Chairman of the Board, which has links to all the groups at NYU.

NYUonline's managers were directly accountable for the company's finances to NYU's vice president for finance, Harold Read, who was also a member of the NYUonline board. Tagliabue prepared a monthly financial report for Read that included the company's financial statements, its current expenses, and provided a projection for next month's expenses. Based on this information, Read transferred the needed funds from an NYU account to NYUonline. Thus, NYU controlled its investment in NYUonline, and had an important accountability lever. Tagliabue was comfortable with this level of financial accountability for NYUonline, especially as a new company: "It is neat that we are in a start-up situation, but we don't have the pressure of capital. NYU is going to make this successful."

This level of accountability highlighted an important difference in operational procedures between NYUonline and NYU. Whereas NYUonline was required to report its expenditures monthly through a formal mechanism, it is almost impossible to imagine monthly financial reports being submitted from academic departments to a dean's office.

At Fathom, all paths of accountability seemed to end at Michael Crow. He was the University's direct contact with the company, representing Columbia on the board of directors and was also considered by many to be chair of the board, though in reality, David Stern, chair of the Columbia board of trustees, was the company's chairman. Kirschner reported directly to Crow and worked closely with him in managing Fathom. Crow, in his position as executive vice provost, reported to Jonathan Cole, Columbia's provost, who in turn reported to George Rupp, Columbia's president. Rupp was not a member of the Fathom board, but noted that he attended most of the board's meetings.

BOARD OF DIRECTORS

The board of directors sits atop the corporate governance hierarchy and is typically composed of seven to nine individuals, including company executives, or "inside directors," and senior executives of similar sized corporations, or "outside directors" (Mace, 1971; NACD, 2000). The board of directors usually serves "as some sort of discipline for the president and his subordinate management" (Mace, 1971, p. 180). In this role, the board serves, with handsome compensation, to oversee management, review the company's finances and allocate funds, ensure compliance with the law, and advise and craft company strategy (Lorsch & MacIver, 1989; Stiles & Taylor, 2001).

In contrast, the board of trustees of a typical private university is composed of 25 to 30 individuals (and sometimes twice as many) who volunteer their time. They not only oversee university management, but are also looked upon as key fundraisers and donors and as advocates and elites to generate community support and trust (W. G. Bowen, 1994). Thus, the board gives the organization legitimacy in the community and with other external constituents.

Board Composition

Each subsidiary's board of directors was structured very differently from its parent's board. The boards of directors were small and included both insiders and outsiders.

NYUonline's board of directors had seven members, four of whom were NYU administrators. The remaining three directors were NYU trustees. (See Table 3–1). None of the NYUonline executives were board members, a departure from standard corporate governance. In contrast to the NYUonline board, the NYU board of trustees had 52 members, with 12 others designated "Life Trustees." This was part of a university governance system Stedman characterized as "complex," with "about eight entities that are sure they are ultimately in charge in academic decision-making." Neither NYU's nor NYUonline's board included a representative of the faculty. According to policy, the Senate "may recommend change to the President, to the Board of Trustees, and to the individual schools" (University Senate, 2001).

Table 3–1. NYUonline Board of Directors

NYUonline Board of Directors (as of June 2001)	Position
Harvey Stedman	NYU Provost
Harold Read	NYU Vice President for Finance
Andy Schaeffer	NYU Senior Vice President and General Counsel
David Finney	Dean, NYU School of Continuing and Professional Studies
William Berkley (chair)*	Trustee; chairman, W.R. Berkley Corporation
Lillian Vernon*	Trustee; CEO, Lillian Vernon Corporation
Kenneth Langone*	Trustee; president & CEO, Invemed Associates, Inc.

* Also members of NYU's Board of Trustees

NYUonline's directors were chosen by NYU's president in consultation with Stedman and Berkley, and approved by NYU's board of trustees. Though he was instrumental in constructing the board, Oliva was not a member of NYUonline's board. Finney noted that excluding NYU's president was designed to distance the president from the company and to give NYUonline an added measure of freedom from the University's governance structure:

> There is a notion that he needed to have just a little distance. . . . Because if the company begins to do something that we all agree is a good idea and it somehow causes the faculty to blow up, the president, as the head of the parent company, needs to have just a little distance so he can actually sit down and talk with the faculty.

Like NYUonline, Babson Interactive's board of directors was structured quite differently from Babson College's board of trustees. The College's board had 31 members; Babson Interactive's had seven. (See Table 3–2.) There were no faculty members on Babson College's board of trustees; Babson Interactive had one. The company also required that two board seats be filled by "outside" directors; however, in practice, these seats were occupied by one outside director, the company's legal counsel, while the other seat was filled by Babson Interactive's chief operating officer. The company's board was appointed by Babson's board of trustees, in concert with Higdon. While Higdon was the sole institutional employee on the College's board, five of the company's seven directors were employed by either Babson College or Babson Interactive, including Higdon.[1]

Table 3–2. Babson Interactive Board of Directors

Babson Interactive Board of Directors (as of June 2001)	Position
Craig Benson (chair)*	Trustee; president & CEO, Cabletron Systems
Ronald Weiner*	Trustee; director in accounting firm
Patricia Guinan	Babson professor, Math & Science department
Leo Higdon, Jr.	President, Babson College
Thomas Moore	CEO, Babson Interactive
James D. Parrino	COO, Babson Interactive; Babson professor
Sharon Goddard White	Chief legal counsel, Babson Interactive

* Also members of Babson College's Board of Trustees

Table 3–3. Duke Corporate Education Board of Directors

Duke CE Board of Directors (as of June 2001)	Position
Douglas Breedan (chair)	Dean, Fuqua School of Business
Peter Lange	Provost, Duke University
Blair Sheppard	CEO, Duke Corporate Education
Tallman Trask III	Exec. Vice President, Duke University

Initially, Duke CE's board was to have seven seats, four for Duke officials and three for outside investors; however, after negotiations broke down with the venture capital firms, no new members were added to the board. (See Table 3–3.) Board members were, in effect, appointed by the Duke CE board itself, with Keohane's approval and ratification by the University's board of trustees. Lange noted that he, Trask, and Breeden selected the board. Trustees were not involved in the process, except to ratify nominations. No University trustees were named as directors. Though Sheppard spoke of the need for an outside voice, none was appointed and the board remained composed of three Duke administrators and Sheppard.

Duke University's board, in contrast, had 37 members[2], all outsiders, with the exception of Keohane. Keohane was not a member of Duke CE's board. She insisted that this was not to maintain separation from the company or "about keeping [her] hands clean."

> I think it's very much a part of my management style and the way this institution works, which is, I have a great deal of faith in my key officers. . . . And on something like this, where they have to get their hands deeply into the details and I don't feel that I have either the time or the need to do that, I really trust them.

Fathom's board reflected the controlling position Columbia had in the consortium of institutions that established the company. Five of the six board members were affiliated with Columbia, with the sixth from the London School of Economics. (See Table 3–4.) Unlike the other three subsidiaries, Fathom's board had only one administrator from the parent institution and half of its members were Columbia trustees, the highest concentration among the four subsidiaries. Indeed, Stern was chair of both boards. Each trustee member of Fathom's board was also a member of a subcommittee to oversee the Universities efforts in "New Media," as online courses, digital material, and other intersections between technology and education were

Table 3–4. Fathom Board of Directors

Fathom Board of Directors (as of June 2001)	Position
Stephen Friedman*	Trustee; Senior Principal, Marsh Capital, Inc.
Alfred Lerner* (passed away, October 2002)	Trustee; Chairman and CEO, MBNA Corp.
David Stern* (chair)	Trustee; Commissioner, National Basketball Association
Michael M. Crow	Executive Vice Provost, Columbia University
Ann Kirschner	President and CEO, Fathom
Keith Mackrell	Chairman, Enterprise LSE; Governor, London School of Economics

* Also members of Columbia University's Board of Trustees

termed by Columbia. This gave Columbia's trustees a visible and important role, not only within Fathom, but in all of Columbia's efforts in this area. Rupp gave the reasons for this structure: "We wanted to make sure that the board of directors of Fathom was controlled by Columbia, and so that's why membership is really dominated by Columbia people."

Rupp was not a member of the subsidiary's board. Like Keohane, he characterized this as a management preference, not an overt attempt to remain independent of the company. Regardless of membership, he was still highly involved: "The fact that I'm not a member? I would have had to ask whether I'm a member or not, because I've been at all the board of directors meeting." In contrast to Fathom's board, Columbia's board of trustees had 24 active members and 39 individuals designated as emeritus trustees. Rupp was the only university employee on Columbia's board.

The differences in board structures indicate that insiders clearly have a much greater voice in governance at the board table of the subsidiaries than is the case in the university. (See Table 3–5.) This reflects corporate practice and also indicates a different view of governance than is the norm for the academy. NYUonline's insider-dominated board, where more than half of the seats are occupied by NYU personnel, is clearly structurally different from NYU's outsider-dominated board. Duke CE's board had no outside representatives. This difference in governance structure indicates a large culture gap between NYU and NYUonline—imagine if NYU administrators filled more than half of the seats on NYU's board of trustees. In traditional academic governance this is unthinkable.

Table 3–5. Comparison of Subsidiary Governing Board Membership

For-profit Subsidiary	# of board members	# of "inside" directors	# of "outside" directors	CEO on board?	President of parent on board?	University board chair on board?
Babson Interactive	7	4	3	Yes	Yes	No
Duke CE	4	4	0	Yes	No	No
Fathom	6	2	4	Yes	No	Yes
NYUonline	7	4	3	No	No	No

The CEO's presence on the board, or lack thereof, signaled a certain degree of cultural congruence between the two organizations. Unlike the other three chief executives, Macomber was not an employee of the university prior to heading NYUonline and had no prior professional connection to academe. At Babson Interactive and Duke Corporate Education, Moore and Sheppard were integral members of the board of directors and enjoyed a relationship of trust with University officials. Their status on the board signaled institutional comfort with their leadership. Kirschner was also a member of Fathom's board. Though not an academic administrator, she was probably benefited from her academic background and career history—a Ph.D. from Princeton and time as a university lecturer—making her presence on Fathom's board less of a threat than Macomber presented at NYU. Of course, Crow's substantial involvement in and oversight of Fathom also may have provided a cultural buffer between Kirschner and Columbia.

Role of the Board in Governance

Financial oversight and concern over clients and partnerships were common themes in the role each subsidiary's board played in governance. Specifically, the boards were concerned with overseeing the parent's investment, monitoring financial performance, and setting constraints to avoid any harmful ramifications the company might have on the university's "brand."

The Duke CE board defined its key role as overseeing the university's financial investment in the company—"watching our money"—as one board member put it. To meet this role, Sheppard reported monthly to the board on three areas: revenues and expenses, the state of the budget, and the company's clients.

Duke CE's board also sought to protect the Duke name. Wallace commented that a key obligation of the company was to "not destroy Duke's brand." The board has made this one of their main concerns, reviewing the company's clients at its monthly meetings, and requiring the company to maintain high standards for its clients and business associates. Even with this oversight, Lange acknowledged that Sheppard and his executive team were "clearly running the shop." He noted that Sheppard had the freedom to act on budgets and operations even though he conferred often with board members.

The role of the Babson Interactive board was not much different. P. J. Guinan, a board member and Babson College professor, stated that the board was concerned with "business decisions," and reviewed the company's revenue projections and costs at quarterly meetings. She asserted that the board's major responsibility was "to make sure that Tom [Moore] is fiscally responsible."

The Babson Interactive board also functioned as a "mechanism of communication" among various College constituents. Laster remarked that the board included trustees, administrators, and faculty in order to allow these three groups to participate in the company's "large decisions." In this sense, the board's role was "to make sure that decision-making in general is appropriate and that communication is flowing back and forth."

Fathom's board provided overall fiscal and operational oversight, monitoring the company's revenues and expenses, approving the budget, and endorsing any additions or changes by Kirschner to the company's executive management group. Aside from these functions, the board's main concerns were (1) to monitor the company's partnerships and business associations in order to protect the University's name and reputation; and (2) to ensure that the company's strategy and operations, according to Rupp, "embody on the Internet what (Columbia) embodies on the ground." Cole articulated this second task as one of ensuring consistency "with the broader mission and goals of the University and our partner institutions." This was accomplished by monitoring Fathom's "specific programs," the overall quality of the company's websites, and its alliances with other businesses.

One of the main concerns of NYUonline's board of directors was the relationship of the subsidiary to the University. In this effort, the board sought to "make sure that it was not out of step with the goals of the University and that the relationship was harmonious."

Other than maintaining that relationship, as Finney asserted, NYUonline's board gave significant operational leeway to Macomber and other NYUonline managers:

> In terms of the actual business strategy and the pursuit of that, . . . they
> have tried not to put any fences around [the company]. They want to give
> [Macomber] room to get a group of people deeply invested in a concept

and make it happen. And I think the University has been committed to allowing him to do that.

The board, however, did approve the subsidiary's business plan and closely monitored and controlled the company's finances by releasing funds to the company on a month-to-month basis.

Relationship between Parent and Subsidiary Board

The relationship between the subsidiary and parent boards varied greatly. On the extremes, Babson College's board of trustees was highly involved in the company's operations, while Duke University's board was quite removed.

At Babson, Fetters claimed that the board's high level of involvement stemmed from the trustees' interest in "protecting their investment." Laster stated that the College's board wanted to "make sure the subsidiary wasn't making commitments that would come back and harm the brand." Guinan asserted that the trustees were interested in "whether or not faculty are happy" and in making sure the company was not "cannibalizing other programs." The close connection to the board of trustees was maintained by having a trustee as chair of the board, through the chair of the college's audit committee, Ron Weiner, who was also a member of the Babson Interactive board. He asserted that the College must be certain that its "risk management, cost, and asset protection plans are honored." To that end, the board of trustees, through its audit committee, required that the College's vice president for finance or vice president for academic affairs review any contract Babson Interactive signed. This practice stemmed from instances, early in the company's existence, when Moore signed agreements for both Babson College and Babson Interactive in his positions as dean of the school of executive education and CEO of Babson Interactive. According to Moore, the board sought to maintain "a clear distinction" between the College and the subsidiary and to ensure "that Babson Interactive wasn't promising things that Babson College had to deliver on." This "screening process," as Moore termed it, was solidified by a clause put in all of the subsidiary's contracts that read, "Babson Interactive speaking for Babson Interactive, not for Babson College." Weiner asserted that this high level of oversight was maintained in order to keep the appropriate relationship between "a for-profit institution that has a classic for-profit governance model . . . [and] subsumed to a certain degree, . . . within the scope of a not for-profit institution, with not for-profit value systems."

Fathom's board was directly connected to Columbia's board through Stern, who was the chair of both. This not only gave Fathom a prominent place in the interest of the Columbia board, but Stern's backing provided a large measure of legitimacy for Fathom. The Columbia board included a subcommittee focused on the University's overall digital media program, including Fathom. Fathom's board also communicated regularly with the trustee's subcommittee on new media. Because of these connections and the trustee's high level of interest, Cole mentioned that in the subsidiary's first two years of operation, the Columbia board was updated at every board meeting on Fathom's operations.

The relationship between NYU's board of trustees and the subsidiary's board was centered on financial accountability for the University's investment. The three NYU trustees on NYUonline's board provided a direct connection between the boards. The NYU board received regular reports from Berkley on the company's prospects.

The Duke board of trustees, perhaps because it did not have a direct link to the company through one of its members seemed to have minimal involvement in Duke CE's governance. However, the board of trustees was updated at least yearly and Keohane communicated regularly with Trask and Lange in order to keep abreast of the company's activities.

FACULTY ROLE IN GOVERNANCE

In governance, faculty are traditionally given responsibility for "curriculum, subject matter and methods of instruction, research, faculty status, and other aspects of student life which relate to the educational process" (AAUP, 1990, p. 5). In these matters, faculty traditionally enjoy primary authority:

> The governing board and president should, on questions of faculty status, as in other matters where the faculty has primary responsibility, concur with the faculty judgment except in rare instances and for compelling reasons which should be stated in detail. (p. 5)

Faculty involvement in governance varied greatly among the four subsidiaries, but overall, was minimal.

Faculty members were not involved in the governance of NYUonline. There were no faculty review bodies to monitor the quality and content of the company's work and professors had only limited review rights over the educational material the company produced. Macomber committed to a faculty advisory board or a board composed of NYU's deans, but did not create one before the company shut down.

Even without involvement in the affairs of NYUonline, NYU faculty seemed to be unconcerned, perhaps because of the University's large size, decentralization, and culture, all of which lead faculty to overlook actions that do not directly affect one's subunit (Clark, 1980). Masland (1991) noted, "Small organizations tend to have stronger cultures than do large organizations. . . . Colleges with highly interdependent parts have stronger cultures than those with autonomous parts" (p. 119). Stedman characterized NYU as more than "a dozen neighborhoods" and as "humongous," "as big as Rhode Island."

Duke CE was paradoxical with respect to faculty governance. Its managers proclaimed that faculty had no role in governance and that "what the [Fuqua] faculty thinks as a collective body is a matter of amusement, not interest." However, managers also deemed the opinions and involvement of individual faculty in the company as "very important." Sheppard claimed that the subsidiary was an egalitarian organization, where the "technical expert is on the same plane or perhaps even more important than the faculty member." However, the title of Academic Director was given to all current or former faculty affiliated with the subsidiary. According to Sitkin, this title referred to "people who possessed depth of expertise in content as well as process." This distinctive title, however, ran contrary to Sheppard's focus on building an egalitarian culture and environment, and seemed to differentiate faculty from other employees. This changed as the subsidiary developed; academic directors became team leaders as the company became more team focused.

Duke CE had no faculty advisory boards, though both Tallman Trask and John Payne, Fuqua's associate dean, mentioned the need for some type of formal faculty group. Sheppard agreed, but did not act. Early in the company's existence, a position on Duke CE's executive committee was reserved for a faculty member. This was originally filled by John McCann, a tenured Fuqua professor, who was Duke CE's Director of Intellectual Curiosity. After a year, McCann rotated off the executive committee and the position was not refilled. Sitkin speculated that the practice was discontinued because company executives felt the position was unnecessary because Sheppard and Gallagher, both professors, were on the committee. Though there was sentiment for and against faculty involvement in governance, the comments of Wanda Wallace summed up the formal role for faculty in Duke CE's governance. She argued that faculty had no oversight role in the company, but were merely "a part of the employee population."

Faculty had a role in governance at Fathom through the Academic Council, an advisory board composed of a representative of each of the consortium affiliates. Most of the Council members were academic administrators, not active professors. Columbia's provost chaired this group. (See Table 3–6.)

Table 3–6. Fathom Academic Council

Fathom Academic Council (as of June 2001)	Position
Jonathan R. Cole, Ph.D. (chair)	Provost, Dean of Faculties, Columbia University
Robert Bud, Ph.D.	Head of Information and Research, Science Museum
John W. Farrington, Ph.D.	Dean of Graduate Studies and Senior Scientist, Woods Hole Oceanographic Institution
Stephen Hill, Ph.D.	Professor and Pro-Director, London School of Economics and Political Science
James Hilton, Ph.D.	Professor, Special Asst. to the Provost for Media Rights, University of Michigan
James Hindman, Ph.D.	Co-Director and COO, American Film Institute
Jeremy Mynott, Ph.D.	CEO, Cambridge University Press
Alice Prochaska, Ph.D.	Director of Special Collections, The British Library
Michael D. Rich, J.D.	Executive VP, RAND
William D. Walker	Senior VP and Director of the Research Libraries, The New York Public Library
Oliver Watson, Ph.D.	Head of the Online Museum, Chief Curator of Ceramics and Glass, The Victoria and Albert Museum
Robert J. Zimmer, Ph.D.	VP for Research and Deputy Provost, University of Chicago

The Academic Council was responsible for setting policy regarding the curricular content offered by Fathom and for overseeing the quality of this material. According to Craig, this council was "a very important governing mechanism for Fathom."

To Crow, faculty involvement in governance was clearly guided by the nature of the subsidiary. Because "faculty are not responsible for the corporate structure of the university," they were not involved in Fathom's strategic or operational decision-making. However, faculty did have review rights and authority over the content they produced for the Fathom website. This arrangement made the subsidiary's governance very clear for Crow: "the faculty's responsibility is related to content, and the board's responsibility is related to structure and legal status."

Even with this supposed clarity in governance, Columbia faculty still had direct influence over Fathom, if only informally. Cole admitted, "Without faculty approval and without faculty buying into this, we don't go forward at all." He commented that generating and maintaining positive faculty opinion of the subsidiary was "very important to us." Crow concurred commenting that "we take heavy account of faculty opinion, faculty trust, and faculty reactions." Part of his job and Cole's was "to keep the faculty happy." Rollow admitted that this affected decision-making: "It ends up affecting decision that the average commercial entity would not be taking into consideration, because they are so worried about the political backlash. Because they are so worried the faculty at Columbia will get upset." This worry over faculty reaction to the subsidiary's decisions was troubling to Kirschner. She admitted that in dealing with faculty, she was "out of [her] element" and was "wistful" for "the clarity of a business decision" that was not overshadowed or influenced by faculty politics.

Faculty involvement in the governance structures and processes of Babson Interactive was limited, yet far greater than at the other subsidiaries. In fact, faculty were quite active in most aspects of the company, a situation that Moore saw as necessary though not ideal. Commenting on Moore's management style, Cohen answered his own questions about Moore: "Would he like to have [Babson Interactive] without faculty control? Sure. Would he like to have it without any faculty participation? No."

At Babson Interactive, faculty were allowed to participate in prescribed roles, but had little control over the non-degree-granting activities of the company; however, in the degree-granting programs offered by Babson Interactive, faculty had significant influence. This came chiefly through two advisory groups, a design committee and an oversight committee. The former examined the design of courses and programs as they were developed, while the latter was responsible for monitoring quality, faculty workload, the rigor and comparability of courses offered by Babson Interactive, and other faculty issues that might arise. Both bodies were sanctioned by and reported to the graduate school's curriculum committee.

In addition to the role faculty played in these governing bodies, a seat on the company's board was reserved for a Babson professor. A professor who was active in delivering the company's programs initially filled this seat. No other subsidiary placed a faculty member on the board.

SOME GENERAL SIMILARITIES

With these data in mind, several generalizations can be distilled, which illuminate the broad similarities in governance among these companies.

1. *The chief executive officer of each for-profit subsidiary had primary internal decision-making authority, yet this authority was not used unilaterally and was quite constrained where the company interacted with the parent or where company actions could reflect upon the parent.*

Whereas governance in the corporation is structured to promote constructive action, the governance of each subsidiary, to varying degrees, was structured to inhibit detrimental action. The managers were constrained in relations with other companies and in their dealings with faculty, thus creating possible obstacles to profitability. These obstacles acted as cultural barriers between each subsidiary and its parent, mitigating the possibility of cultural contamination. Even at Fuqua and Babson College, institutions where business and entrepreneurship are a way of life, the constraints imposed by directors signaled that the company was seen as a possible, however slight, risk to each parent's reputation and operation. With these constraints, each subsidiary's CEO was not all-powerful as faculty may have feared.

2. *Decisions were made faster in the subsidiaries, though the hoped for speed and independence in decision-making was not achieved.*

None of the subsidiaries was able to totally separate itself from the ponderous processes of shared governance. Each parent articulated speed as a reason for creating the company as a separate subsidiary, yet none maximized this objective.

Decisions were certainly made faster in the subsidiaries than by traditional universities; however, this seemed due in part to the internal authority of the CEO and also to the small size of each company. Even if a leader desired a great amount of input into a decision, it did not take much time to consult widely because of the size of each company.

The drop-off in decision-making speed came when the subsidiary interacted with its parent. Moore had to talk with Fetters regarding faculty use and program design. Fathom had to pass through the Columbia bureaucracy to send email to university alumni.

3. *Decision-making largely reflected business concerns, e.g., client satisfaction, profit / financial considerations, and protection of university brand; however, this was not absolute.*

These subsidiaries were businesses, with profit remaining a key goal. Many of the principles upon which decisions were made reflected this. In large part, business guided decisions. Yet, the protection of the parent institution's brand name was elevated past typical profit and loss concerns. No company was willing or allowed to "make a buck" at the expense of the parent institution. Though Reinheimer stated that client satisfaction was the central criteria in Duke CE's decisions, first clients had to be deemed acceptable. Similar restrictions were in place at the other subsidiaries. Thus, profit was subservient to the good of the parent institution.

4.   *In contrast to the clarity of intra-organizational accountability and reporting relationships, inter-organizational accountability was convoluted and often conflicted.*

Within the administrative structure of a typical university, reporting relationships and lines of accountability are clear and unquestioned; however, this clarity diminishes drastically when the academic structure is considered. Likewise, internal accountability in each subsidiary's governance was straightforward, yet became muddled between the board of directors, university administration, and board of trustees.

5.   *Each subsidiary's board was structured and functioned to reduce the harmful effects of actions by the subsidiary on the parent institution and provide legitimacy for the subsidiary.*

The subsidiary's boards may have been structured with an eye towards company performance, but were clearly structured with the protection of the parent in mind. The board's role, which for most companies was appropriately one of oversight, was driven by a desire to mitigate negative effects on the parent, either financially or reputationally.

6.   *Faculty involvement in governance varied, from no involvement to membership on an advisory board or a seat on the board of directors.*

Consistent with the desire to operate independent of the parent institution's governance structure, faculty were largely excluded from formal participation in governance. Babson Interactive was the notable exception because of its reserved seat for a faculty member on its board. The substantial informal influence faculty had on these companies will be considered in chapter 5.

HYBRIDS AND CULTURAL COMPATIBILITY

The environment in which each subsidiary operated produced similarities in governance structure and process, a phenomenon called isomorphism, where organizations come to resemble others with the same set of environmental circumstances (DiMaggio & Powell, 1991; Gates, 1997). The subsidiaries operated in a for-profit environment financially, which shaped their internal governance and decision-making. "Financial behavior defines organizational behavior" (Slaughter & Leslie, 1997, p. 66). Their boards were small and filled with both insiders and outsiders, their CEOs held significant authority, and each company's internal reporting relationships were clear and ordered. These subsidiaries possessed many corporate characteristics, quite different from their parents. This differentiation facilitated interaction with the broader business environment (J. D. Thompson, 1967). As David Hawthorne, senior vice president at NYUonline, remarked: "We created a business-friendly user interface by giving [corporations] a company that deals like a business, that has the look and feel of a business, and that they can talk to like a business."

However, these subsidiaries also operated within the orbit of each parent institution's culture as well. This "magnetic field" reduced the degree of corporatization in each subsidiary. Because culture "establishes an 'envelope'" of structural and behavioral possibilities "within which the organization usually functions" (Birnbaum, 1988, p. 73), the parent institutions' cultural boundaries restricted each subsidiary from venturing too far from established procedure and behavior. Thus, these subsidiaries became governance hybrids, incorporating aspects of the academy and corporation. The degree of hybridization in each subsidiary was moderated by the parent culture.

Notwithstanding the broad similarities among the subsidiaries, there were more important differences. If arranged on a continuum, Babson Interactive would be closer to the governance structures and processes typified by academic governance and NYUonline closer to corporate governance. (See Figure 3–1.) Duke CE and Fathom would fall near the middle, with Duke CE showing more similarity to the traditional structures and processes of academic governance than Fathom.

Because academic culture is very powerful (Birnbaum, 1988; H. R. Bowen & Schuster, 1986), the cultural differences between the parent and subsidiary affected each company's governance. The degree of difference culturally was small for Babson Interactive and so it functioned almost like a regular department in the College, with Moore directing it as he would an academic unit. Fathom's managers were much more careful because the difference in cultures was much greater. Academic culture influenced these managers to take great care in their interactions with Columbia and in the way they marketed the company's material. Sheppard employed academic characteristics into the decision-processes of Duke CE and many of its managers sought collaboration and consultation in decision-making. The company was established to create separation from Fuqua, but many of its processes were much like its parent.

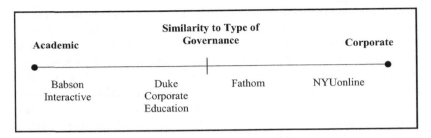

Figure 3–1. Governance Continuum

At NYU, the difference was quite pronounced. There seemed to be a concern about having the company too close to the operations and culture of the University, as if NYUonline could contaminate the environment or be rejected by the "host organ." Stedman remarked that NYUonline needed a "separation from the historical protocols of the [University]. So that it could make its own way with less of the entanglement of the place." Finney commented:

> In terms of the divergent cultures, yes, I think it is important to keep the company at arm's length, and that is why it is structured the way it is. I mean, from any faculty member's experience on campus here, the existence of this company has meant nothing, other than perhaps some money for content that they've provided to it.

The for-profit nature and operation of the subsidiary also seemed to cause concern. Finney noted:

> [NYUonline] has a general tendency to want to be a little more aggressive and quicker to market than a university tends to move. Which is one of the reasons why it's an outside company, out of the bureaucracy. They aren't necessarily as careful with academic terms, like 'course' and 'faculty member,' and that worries regulatory agencies, because they are not an educational institution.

Babson Interactive and Duke CE were more academic in governance because each subsidiary's culture aligned better with its parent's culture than did Fathom and NYUonline. In essence, Babson Interactive was a better fit with Babson College than NYUonline was with NYU. Reframing the governance continuum as a measure of the "fit" between each subsidiary and its parent's culture would yield the same distribution of institutions, with Babson Interactive most compatible and NYUonline least. (See Figure 3–2.)

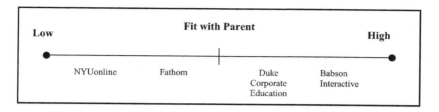

Figure 3–2. Cultural Fit Continuum

SUMMING UP

Several conclusions can be drawn from the governance of these subsidiaries.

- The subsidiaries were governance hybrids, with aspects and characteristics of both governance traditions.
- In the subsidiaries, governance served to limit scope and "reign," whereas in the corporate sector, governance is employed toward action—to make things happen. These governance constraints were meant to "protect" the parent institution and restrain the actions of the subsidiary in order to avoid violating the cultural values of the parent institution.
- Though each subsidiary desired separation from its parent's governance structures and processes, complete separation was never achieved. This resulted not from the mechanisms employed, but because of the power of academic culture.
- Because governance and culture are so intertwined, circumventing governance means circumventing culture—or at least attempting to. And the degree of separation in governance is a reflection of cultural compatibility. Two cultures that cannot profitably coexist will be isolated from each other.
- Finally, returning to the parallel between the for-profit subsidiary and a business merger or acquisition, in mergers and acquisitions, as Schein (1999) asserts, "An acquisition strategy has to fit the existing culture (p. 32). A similar statement might be made for the for-profit subsidiary of the nonprofit university. Cultural compatibility is an important consideration in the creation and governance of these companies.

Chapter Four
Personnel Connections: Culture Creation and Mediation in the Subsidiaries

The for-profit subsidiaries differ from their parent institutions to varying degrees. They "have a different tone from the rest of the university." Speaking of Fathom, the *Washington Post Magazine* described the differences, only partly attributable to the fact that "Fathom's offices are half a city downtown from Columbia's main campus—80 blocks south of the marble edifices and manicured quads of Morningside Heights" (Shea, 2001, September 16).

> The company occupies an upper floor in a building that squats in the shadow of the Empire State Building, just around the corner from Korea-town. Its offices lack the usual interior-decorating scheme of an old, exclusive college: no wood paneling, no Colonial chairs, no oil paintings of gray-haired eminent men from eras past staring into the middle distance.
>
> No, Fathom is conspicuously modern. The reception area comes straight from the Silicon Alley playbook: a crisp green floor, touches of unfinished metal here and there, daunting sculptural chairs that cordially invite you to remain standing. A spiral staircase leads down into a loft-y looking space, in which three dozen young people type and surf away in a cubicleless nirvana. (p. W25)

Duke CE's physical space is quite similar to Fathom's. Immediately after creating the company, Sheppard moved it from the Fuqua School to a century old, red brick, tobacco warehouse in downtown Durham, far from the idyllic forest and secluded setting of the University. Initially, Duke CE occupied the building's existing functional space, with workspace in several large rooms over three floors. These undivided rooms held everyone in the company, from Sheppard to the secretaries, who all sat at identical desks with the same arrangements. Rather than a corner office, Sheppard merely occupied a corner of this large room. This egalitarian workspace was consistent with the goals of both Sheppard and Wallace, who desired to create an atmosphere where all employees were valued equally.

However, while creating this environment, they made plans to renovate and refurbish an entire wing of the building for the company's future home. The red brick exterior stayed, but the interior of the building was transformed into an edifice of modern furniture, dark wood, and high technology. Most of the workspace was still left undivided and open, though Sheppard now resides in a secluded office on the building's top floor. In contrast to the white walls and individual offices of the Fuqua School, Duke CE tried to create the "work hard, play hard" atmosphere of a dot com company by building a back deck, complete with a barbecue grill, onto the building's lower level adjacent to a kitchen and dining area. The building's colors were vibrant and energizing and the company's employees always seemed in motion. There were no closed doors and no one worked in isolation. The company's website described its location and character:

> Duke Corporate Education is a hybrid—a cross between a business and a university. If you visit us at our headquarters in Durham, North Carolina you will find us neither on campus (a short distance away) nor in a traditional office building. We work in a recently renovated historic tobacco warehouse. Each person's workspace is identical to the next one in size and furniture. Partitions are low. The rooms are large with tall ceilings. The space reflects who we are—open and collaborative. (DukeCE, 2003)

The workspace arrangement, décor, and locale of each of these companies—all cultural artifacts—were also signals, at Schein's first level of culture, that equally striking differences existed between the basic assumptions and espoused values of the parent and subsidiary. In artifacts, "culture is clear and has immediate emotional impact" (Schein, 1999, p. 16). The artifacts, created and arranged by each subsidiary's founding personnel and key leaders, were visual indicators of the difference between the culture of the parent and subsidiary. In fact, even the physical separation of these companies from campus foreshadowed a larger cultural separation.

In contrast to this separation at Duke and Columbia, Babson Interactive never moved off campus, and for over a year, Moore managed the company from his office in Babson's Graduate School of Business. Again, culture was at work here, however it was not only the culture of the parent institution that made for sharp contrast at Duke CE and Fathom, but the budding cultures of the subsidiaries, forged by each company's founders and key personnel.

This chapter first examines the role of personnel in the formation of culture in a new or young organization and then details the four different personnel arrangements of each subsidiary, with a special focus on the chief executive. I then discuss the overt attempts by several subsidiaries to create a hybrid culture through its personnel, by incorporating aspects from business and academe. Finally, I examine the mediating role played by key personnel between the parent and subsidiary and then conclude with a discussion of cultural leadership in these subsidiaries.

CULTURE FORMATION IN YOUNG ORGANIZATIONS

The values, assumptions, and beliefs of a new organization's founders and early leaders are a key source of culture. Leaders of a new or young organization have unsurpassed influence on its future culture. In new organizations, "culture begins with leaders who impose their own values and assumptions on a group" (Schein, 1992, p. 1). The influence of founders is so profound that often, even in mature companies, many cultural assumptions, organizational values, or processes can be traced to the influence of a founder or early leader.

People enter newly formed organizations with "values and thought patterns . . . partially determined by their own cultural backgrounds and their shared experience" (Schein, 1999, p. 14). Because an organization's founders usually produce the guiding idea for the organization, "they will typically have their own notion, based on their own cultural history and personality, of how to fulfill the idea" (Schein, 1992, p. 212–213). These cultural histories—values, thought patterns, learned behaviors, and experiences—imposed on subsequent personnel and perpetuated and magnified through hiring people who share these values and experiences, lay the foundation of the organization's culture. With continued organizational success, these shared values and assumptions become taken for granted—"tacit rules of how to do things" (p. 26)—and are passed on through the socialization of new organizational members (Corcoran & Clark, 1984; Etzioni, 1975; Kuh & Whitt, 1988; Schein, 1992, 1999). The process of cultural formation is very important to a young organization; in fact, culture has been called a new organization's "primary asset" (Schein, 1999, p. 92).

An organization's founding personnel transmit their values and beliefs in what they pay attention to and measure, how they react to critical incidents and crises, and in the criteria by which other organizational participants are selected, rewarded, or punished. These primary cultural embedding mechanisms are supported by secondary mechanisms that serve to articulate and reinforce values and beliefs. These include the design of physical space and buildings, the stories and myths that are told and retold about people or events, and formal mission statements or organizational creeds (Schein, 1999; Schein, 1992).

Each of these mechanisms contributes to the new organization's culture, yet perhaps the most important cultural determinants are the behaviors and ideas of an organization's founders and early leaders (Schein, 1999, p. 99). In effect, leaders become "living embodiments" of the new culture (Kotter & Heskett, 1992, p. 146). Founders provide answers to group members' questions about how to operate, and if successful, these solutions are repeated and passed on to new group members. If the founders and early leaders are not successful in solving early organizational problems or crises, other leaders will step forward. If these new leaders help the organization succeed, their values, beliefs, and preferred actions will be perpetuated through the socialization of new members, thus culture is born and perpetuated.

Schein (1992) contends that the process of cultural creation is the very "essence of leadership" and that "leadership and culture are two sides of the same coin" (p. 1). Perhaps this is overstated for mature organizations, but in the cultural vacuum of young organizations, the imposition of the values and beliefs of founding personnel is a key to cultural development.

In contrast to the cultural incubation stage a new organization goes through, mature organizational cultures often reject leadership that is not consistent with its assumptions and values. Only certain types of leaders are accepted in culturally mature organizations. Schein (1992) asserts:

> Once an organization has evolved a mature culture because it has a long and rich history, that culture creates the patterns of perception, thought, and feeling of every new generation in the organization, and, therefore, also "causes" the organization to be predisposed to certain kinds of leadership. (p. 313)

In this way, "the mature group, through its culture, also creates its own leaders" (Schein, 1992, p. 313). Thus, culture influences leadership just as powerfully as leadership influences culture. "What institutions have done in the past may therefore have a profound influence over what their leaders can do today" (Birnbaum, 1992, p. 160).

This has particular relevance in the case of for-profit subsidiaries. Though each subsidiary is in effect a new entity, with founding leaders whose beliefs and values shape the organization, each subsidiary is also connected to a parent organization with a mature culture that is predisposed to a certain type of leadership, and thus, has a measure of cultural control over the subsidiary's leadership. Often, "the culture issue is blatant and visible" (Schein, 1999, p. 8), when two organizations come together in a merger or joint venture. In these situations, the risk of cultural mismatch and thus organizational failure are equally high. For leaders to be effective, they must align their strategies with the dominant culture, rather than compete with it (Chaffee & Tierney, 1988). If they are not able to do this, the dominant institution may reject them and their organization as well. Thus, "the single most visible factor that distinguishes major cultural changes that succeed from those that fail, is competent leadership" (Kotter & Heskett, 1992, p. 84).

Consistent with Schein's (1992) assertion that "in young organizations one must focus primarily on leadership behavior to understand cultural growth" (p. 254), the next two sections examine each subsidiary's founding personnel, particularly the chief executive and his or her role in cultural formation.

LEADERS IN THE SUBSIDIARIES

Each parent institution followed a different course choosing the personnel for its subsidiary. Columbia and NYU hired "outsiders" with little or no previous connection to the parent university. Babson and Duke, conversely, hired "insiders." Whether insiders or outsiders, these CEOs then set out to create an organization, chiefly through hiring personnel, which reflected their view of the company's purpose and strategy for success, but also reflected their backgrounds, values, and beliefs.

On August 16, 2000, Tom Moore was appointed CEO of Babson Interactive. At the time, Moore was dean of both Babson's graduate school of business and the school of executive education. With his appointment, Moore resigned as dean of the graduate school of business, but retained his position in executive education. As one newspaper put it, with these two positions, "he will straddle both the non-profit and profit-making worlds in what could become a model for other B-schools" (MBANewsletter, 2000, p. 1).

As dean of two schools at Babson, Moore had proven his ability to bring about change in an academic environment when he led the successful revision of Babson's curriculum in the early 1990's. In fact, Professor Allan Cohen said Moore was hired as Babson Interactive's CEO because he "gets things done." Because of his experience and administrative abilities, Moore was highly regarded and trusted by both faculty and administrators.

P. J. Guinan, a professor of information technology and member of the company's board of directors, remarked that hiring Moore made "good business sense, . . . because Tom is so connected with the College." She felt that Moore's long relationship with and commitment to Babson would make him "more careful with the money . . . because Tom knows perfectly well that if [the company] doesn't work out he's going to be at Babson for a long time." Guinan was confident that because of this relationship, Moore would never do anything that might endanger the College. Fred Nanni, a professor of accounting, argued that an outsider would not have fit in at the helm of Babson Interactive:

> If they brought in somebody from outside I don't think that that would have flown quite as well, because that in itself clashes with the way that we do things. It's not a Babson way of doing things. The Babson way of doing things is to find someone who's got the skills internally and is trusted as a known commodity.

Joining Moore at Babson Interactive was Stephen Laster, who was named chief technology officer. Laster held an MBA degree from Babson, and, as Moore noted, "knows curriculum," "knows how to teach," and, perhaps most importantly, "knows Babson." Jim Parrino, an associate professor of finance at Babson with extensive experience in executive education, was named chief operating officer, while also retaining his faculty appointment. All other Babson Interactive employees either had been or were currently employed by the College or were alumni.

Blair Sheppard, Fuqua's senior associate dean for academic programs and a tenured professor, was named president and CEO of Duke Corporate Education on July 1, 2000. Sheppard held a Ph.D. in social and organizational psychology from the University of Illinois and was an expert in corporate strategy, negotiation, and organizational design. As Fuqua's senior associate dean, Sheppard was one of the chief architects of two successful management education programs, the Global Executive MBA and the Cross-Continent MBA. Both programs combined distance-learning technology with traditional classroom education to enable students from all over the world to come to Durham. These programs helped create the technology Duke CE later adopted to deliver its customized corporate education (DukeCE, 2000c).

Joining Sheppard at Duke CE was Wanda Wallace, Fuqua's associate dean for executive education; John Gallagher, a Fuqua professor, key architect of the School's highly successful Global Executive MBA program, and director of its Computer Mediated Learning Center and newly formed e-Learning Solutions group; and John McCann, a tenured professor at Fuqua who specialized in e-commerce (Panus, 2000, June 30). These three filled the titles, respectively, of executive vice president of educational programs, vice president of learning technology and development, and director of intellectual curiosity. With Sheppard, they formed the company's executive committee.

In addition, all employees of Fuqua's customized executive education program joined Duke CE. As an incentive, each new employee received ownership shares (Chronicle, 2000), which totaled 20 percent of the company's equity (DukeCE, 2000a). The company's website proclaimed this as one of Duke CE's strengths, "enabling [them] to attract and hold top-quality people" using "equity-based incentives" (DukeCE, 2003). Despite these incentives, many of Duke CE's employees were still paid through the University in order to retain retirement and other University benefits and employment seniority. Sheppard resigned his tenure at Fuqua to head Duke CE, while McCann retained his tenure and took a two-year leave from the School.

Ann Kirschner was already employed by Columbia University when on April 3, 2000, she was named president and CEO of Fathom (Goldman, 2000). Kirschner, however, had only been with the University a short time, hired by Michael Crow in 1999, to "create a company that would develop strategies and businesses to maximize the benefits" of Columbia's intellectual properties. Ryan Craig, who was completing his law degree at Columbia and had helped with the formation of the company, was named Fathom's vice president for business development.

Though Kirschner was an accomplished business executive, her background was unlike that of a typical corporate CEO. She held a Ph.D. in English literature from Princeton University and had worked for the Modern Language Association. However, because of the scarcity of academic jobs, she turned to business and the budding cable industry. After successfully creating and selling her own satellite television company, she was tabbed to create the website for the National Football League, which she built into the most popular website of any professional sporting league. From NFL.com she joined Columbia and Michael Crow to head Morningside Ventures, an organization founded by Crow (Carlson, 2000b).

Fathom's "senior team," as Kirschner called the company's key executives, included Craig; David Wolff, vice president of programming and production; a chief financial officer; and a chief technology officer. Besides Craig, only the chief technology officer, Bill Ying, who received master's and doctoral degrees from Columbia, had a direct link to the University (Fathom, 2000). As Kirschner admitted, "No one else has any Columbia affiliation." Similarly, her own ties to the institution were limited: "My Columbia affiliation is my daughter is graduating from Barnard this year, my husband trained in the neurological institute at the medical school, and I once took a summer course in German." Crow stated that Kirschner was hired for her "dual background in academe and business."

> The average business person is the take-no-prisoners type, with no soft
> touch. But she has the right touch, the right skill to work within the aca-
> demic context. She has the right commitment to intellectual rigor. . . .
> She shows that she understands academic culture. She knows that she's
> not sitting across the table from U.S. Steel. (Carlson, 2000b)

Craig left Fathom in 2001 to join Warburg Pincus, a venture capital firm.
Anne Rollow, a recent graduate of the Harvard Business School who also
had no previous affiliation with Columbia, replaced him.

Gerald Heeger, then dean of NYU's School of Professional and
Continuing Studies, championed the creation of NYUonline, in October
1998. However, coincident with the company's creation, Heeger left NYU
to become the president of the University of Maryland University College.
David Finney was appointed to replace Heeger as dean and was also initially
selected to lead the new company, along with several other NYU administrators who had expertise in technology and distance education. These individuals managed the company for the first year of its existence, creating its
first online courses (Letterman, 1999, October 20). However, in January
2000, NYUonline's board of directors hired Gordon Macomber, a veteran
media publisher and e-commerce executive, as president and CEO.

Three months later, Macomber brought on "six seasoned profession-
als" to fill the company's top management positions. These positions included vice president of marketing and communications, chief information
officer, senior vice president of strategic marketing, senior vice president of
global business development, vice president of learning support, and senior
vice president of e-learning. Macomber characterized the appointment of
these managers as "mission critical" to establishing NYUonline as an industry leader (Kocijan, 2000, March 27).

Though several of these new managers had some experience in educational institutions—one was a certified teacher, another taught high school,
and another held a masters degree in special education—only one held a degree from NYU, a bachelor's in journalism. Four of the six held either a law
degree or an MBA and had served as either president or CEO of a company
before coming to NYUonline. In essence, they were business executives with
expertise in finance, marketing, publishing, and technology (Kocijan, 2000,
March 27). To advertise the arrival of these executives, the company's website proclaimed, "Like your company, NYUonline is a for-profit business,
comprised of a top management team committed to meeting your strategic
e-Learning goals" (NYUonline, 2001).

NYUonline hired Macomber to try to achieve the market success that
was envisioned for the company. Macomber, who held a bachelor's degree

in economics, had no background in academe, but had experienced considerable success as an entrepreneur and executive in the electronic and print publishing industries. As an entrepreneur, he had founded a company that helped authors and publishers develop written content for the Internet. Prior to that, as the president of Macmillan Reference USA, he helped two divisions of the company move from print to online, and before that, was vice president for emerging markets in another MacMillan company. Of Macomber's qualifications for the job, Finney noted:

> Gordon combines outstanding executive management experience with groundbreaking vision. I am confident that he will successfully lead NYUonline's mission to combine state-of-the-art technology with up-to-date content and the accumulated knowledge and pedagogical tradition of NYU in a never-before-seen interactive format. (Kocijan, 2000, January 3)

Bill Berkley, chair of the NYUonline board, commented on the importance of hiring Macomber:

> NYU has a tremendous brand name in continuing education. We are ecstatic to bring Gordon on board to help NYUonline leverage the NYU brand and offer superior online education to individuals, corporations and other educational institutions. (Kocijan, 2000, January 3)

Macomber considered it an advantage in running the company that his professional background was entirely outside of higher education. He asserted that while being allowed "into the inner sanctum of the University," he "distinctively did not bring to them a perspective ground in academia." He recognized and stated emphatically that he was at NYUonline "because [it was] on the outside."

CREATING A NEW CULTURE

Using Schein's (1992) theory on cultural formation in young organizations, one could guess that the four subsidiaries would develop different cultures because of the differences in their early leaders. Each subsidiary would develop in accord with the values and beliefs held by its leaders, mediated by the culture of the parent organization, and thus form divergent cultures.

The leaders of two subsidiaries worked to create new cultures, in order to function effectively at the intersection of business and academe. Duke CE and Fathom officials spoke of creating a "hybrid organization" that could interact equally well with professors on one hand and corporate clients on the other. This type was not mentioned at Babson Interactive. NYUonline recognized the importance of communication and a good relationship with NYU, but seemed to reject incorporating any aspects of the University into the subsidiary.

Led by Sheppard, Duke CE sought to consciously create a new culture with "the excellence of a university and the values of a commercial enterprise." In this pursuit, Duke CE rejected elements of both cultures that were seen as potentially detrimental to the success of the company or that did not seem to square with the values of the founders. Though Sheppard was a former tenured Fuqua professor and administrator, he was highly critical of the faculty-centered culture of academe and worked hard at Duke CE to alter it. This was apparent in the use of terminology to describe personnel in the company. As I spoke with several of the subsidiary's founders, I was continually and often emphatically corrected when I used the term "faculty" to describe Fuqua professors who now worked with Duke CE. Wanda Wallace illustrated, "Whoa, whoa, whoa. No. No, no, no. Wrong mantra, totally wrong mantra. Employees. All of us are employees. We will not create this faculty versus staff dichotomy." Within Duke CE, professors were "employees" and "academics" and not faculty. And it was clear that the dichotomy, as Wallace stated, which clearly they believed started with titles, would not be replicated at Duke CE. John Gallagher underscored Wallace's point:

> The faculty run Fuqua, but the academics don't run Duke Corporate Education. This is not a replication of a university culture in that sense. They are academics but they are not faculty in the sense that they are the ones who run the organization. That having been said, almost everyone in a position of any authority has a history as a faculty member and an academic.

Gallagher's qualifier is key. Largely due to the background of most of the leading personnel in the company, at least at its founding, the company, according to Gallagher, still "feels a lot like a university."

However, this feel was something that Sheppard sought to alter. In order to "break the traditional mind-set" of company personnel, Sheppard set out to hire top leaders from the corporate world and to sprinkle corporate personnel throughout the subsidiary. The most visible example was the hiring, closely following the company's founding, of Judy Rosenblum, an executive with Coca-Cola and a corporate organizational learning expert. By bringing in Rosenblum, and later others from the corporate sector who had no previous affiliation with Duke or Fuqua, Sheppard hoped to create "a kind of unholy marriage," as he termed it, "a balance between the academic world and the business world." By achieving this balance, Sheppard hoped to form a company that was "a hybrid," whose culture would be "highly distinct from Fuqua's." He theorized that this would attract corporate clients who were more comfortable working with a business, but who also wanted the quality education the Duke name represented. The results of Sheppard's work were displayed prominently on Duke CE's website in an attempt to attract corporate clients: "We have combined academics, educators, and executives from the corporate learning environments to create a uniquely powerful array of talent to address your company's needs." (DukeCE, 2000b) Similar to Duke CE, Kirschner sought to create a different type of organization. The idea of bringing two cultures together through Fathom's personnel was apparent in her description of the company's employees:

> We're like the best group of graduate students you've ever studied with. Which is to say that it's a highly intellectual and academically accomplished group of people who love the university and love the content that we develop at Fathom. At the same time, it's like a bright group of young investment bankers who seek great opportunities and who are fearless in going forward.

In fact, Kirschner embodied this combination. Rupp described Kirschner as "a Ph.D. in English from Princeton and sort of a cerebral sort" and commented that she was "not only a gun slinging MBA trying to make a lot of money, but [someone who] really has interest in some of the intellectual qualities of the University." Rupp commented, however, that Kirschner was hired to "see things differently" than the Columbia administration.

Kirschner's different outlook may have caused some difficulties. Even with her academic credentials, one professor remarked that Kirschner was "offensive" because of her corporate background and commented that someone who had a history with Columbia and no connection to the corporate world would have been a better fit for Fathom. Cole, Columbia's provost, also seemed to feel that early on, Fathom had gone too far in hiring from the business world and had employed too many of what he called the "young hot shots in this business." This was later remedied when Fathom restructured to eliminate its marketing department. When this happened, many of these early employees left the company. Cole remarked that this process was important in "changing the culture of the people" who were with the company to focus more on the quality of Fathom's materials and less on developing the company and its website. Kirschner admitted that this restructuring was necessary in order to "avoid tilting [the company] too much from one side to the other."

NYUonline did not try to incorporate aspects of NYU's culture, in fact, the company's managers seemed to actively reject the University's cultural and organizational characteristics. One NYUonline executive proclaimed emphatically, "We are not the University," and then listed the many differences between the two organizations. He asserted that being different from the University was essential to the company's success.

> The last thing corporations wanted to deal with when it came to providing training and education for their employees, was universities. . . . So in that sense, structurally, a business or for-profit entity was essential. So we created a business friendly user interface by giving them a company that deals like a business, that has the look and feel of a business, and that they can talk to like a business.

Similarly, Finney noted that the company needed "to have a little distance" from the University in order to operate effectively. This distance seemed to also include keeping aspects of the University's culture away from NYUonline and vice versa. He remarked, "In terms of the divergent cultures, yes, I think it is important to keep the company at arm's length, and that is why it is structured the way it is."

Maintaining a business culture by staffing the company only with business personnel, according to David Daniel, NYUonline's chief information officer, was crucial to its early success. He remarked that this "was what really mattered:"

> What matters is do they try to do it with business people or do they try to do it with a bunch of university administrators. I mean, the reason we're having a lot of success right now, . . . is everybody on the team is a very experienced businessman.

Daniel was so sure of this that he predicted that similar subsidiaries managed by academic administrators would fail:

> They're mostly just trying to pick some guy at the university who knows a little more about technology than the next guy and make him run it. And that's a big mistake. They're going to get nailed doing that, because you've got to understand business to make this work.

Consistent with this philosophy, NYUonline rejected the idea of creating a hybrid organization and instead built an organization dominated by business people. Its desire to keep the company separate from the University was not always possible, however, and some conflicts developed. Robert Manuel, an NYU administrator commented:

> NYU and NYUonline definitely speak a different language, which can create some problems. NYU talks about students and NYUonline talks about populations or markets and consumers. They are referring to the same thing, but using vastly different terms. Sometimes this doesn't go over too well with faculty.

Correspondingly, Finney noted that NYUonline was created as a separate company because, "They aren't necessarily as careful with academic terms, like course and faculty member. And this worries faculty and it worries regulatory agencies." These concerns drove both NYU and NYUonline to carefully maintain the separation between the organizations. NYUonline stuck to business and its board of directors continued to try to keep an appropriate "distance" between the two organizations. Macomber remarked, "We are running in the classic business style and to some degree, it has to be run that way."

Like NYUonline, Babson Interactive also did not try to create a hybrid organization. However, instead of creating a pure corporate entity, Babson Interactive was created as an extension of the College's culture. In contrast to NYUonline, Moore felt it "would be a major disadvantage" if Babson Interactive "operated at arm's length" with Babson College. Moore wanted "direct contact" between the company and the College and worked to "integrate Babson Interactive back to the graduate school and the school of executive education." To accomplish this Moore hired company personnel who had a high level of familiarity with the College and were comfortable working with faculty and administrators.

"One of the most decisive functions of leadership is the creation . . . of culture" (Schein, 1992, p. 5), and "when a company hires a CEO, they also hire a culture" (Sansalone, 2000). This was the case with each subsidiary. Each company's board hired the CEO and that person in turn created the culture of the subsidiary according to his values and beliefs and what he felt would make the company most successful. Macomber isolated NYUonline from NYU; Moore integrated Babson Interactive with Babson College; Sheppard and Kirschner tried to create a hybrid, with connections between parent and subsidiary in some respects and separation in others.

THE MEDIATOR'S ROLE

In order to manage what most felt was a crucial connection between the subsidiary and its parent, each pair of organizations, in different ways, established a central contact between them. Speaking specifically of a leader's role in bringing two companies with different cultures together through a merger or acquisition, Schein (1992) argued that organizational personnel could serve as a "buffering layer" (p. 230) between the two organizations, particularly when values and beliefs clashed. The idea of a mediator between two organizations that have different purposes or functions is not new, especially as many companies have recently created separate organizations, distinct from their core operating units, to either benefit from technology or minimize the negative effect of a "disruptive technology" on their core business (Christensen, 1997). Gilbert and Bower (2002, May), reporting on a study of newspaper corporations that created separate Internet units, argued that this mediator—either a person (or small group)—should ideally be an executive in the parent organization who possesses a great deal of autonomy and high credibility in both organizations. The role of this "active integrator" is to "manage the tensions between the parent and the new venture" (p. 100). Bower (1970) noted that a mediator of this type is pivotal in the management of change and particularly in the integration of two company's processes and structures. Along with helping to resolve conflict, smooth communication, and maintain the resource commitment between the organizations (Gilbert, 2001), the mediator's "crucial role" is to "take advantage of the tensions and synergies that emerge" from the two organizations as they relate to each other yet operate in different contexts (Tushman, Anderson, & O'Reilly, 1997, p. 19).

Crow acted as a mediator between Columbia and Fathom. Kirschner also helped, as did Cole, who advocated for Fathom's interests from his position as provost. However, Crow was the primary mediator because of his role on Fathom's board, his position and standing within Columbia, and his direct responsibility for many of the University's entrepreneurial ventures. As Rupp remarked, Crow was "the embodiment of the entrepreneurial streak at Columbia" and was an effective advocate of the University's push into the production of digital educational material and its distribution online through Fathom. Yet, as a Ph.D. and former professor himself, he also understood faculty culture and could speak to faculty with a high degree of credibility.

For problems or "road blocks" Fathom encountered in its work, Crow was the immediate source of advice or solutions. Rollow commented that Crow was often called on to help with "political maneuvering" between the two organizations. He also acted as a cultural interpreter and guide for Fathom personnel in working with Columbia. According to Rollow, she and others at Fathom would ask him questions, such as:

> Is this the only way we can do this? Is there someone else we can talk to? Is there some other way to work this through? What are we not understanding about the culture that is causing the problem here? Why can't we do it this way? How should we do it?

Crow's answers helped reveal possible pitfalls and hazards Fathom should avoid in its relationship with Columbia.

More often, Crow did not just answer questions, but actively advocated for Fathom with Columbia's constituencies. In the fall of 2000, Columbia's University Senate created a joint subcommittee of its Budget, Education, External Relations, and Student Affairs Committees to address a "number of concerns that individual faculty raised about the University's overall Internet strategy in general, and about Fathom in particular." An opinion in the campus newspaper articulated one of these concerns:

> It is very ironic that a university that claims never to have enough money for clearly needed academic enhancements—i.e., more faculty for an increased number of undergraduates—would be so willing to throw money at something whose benefits are unlikely, if ever, to materialize. (Lowe, 2002, February 7)

The joint subcommittee's focus on Fathom received a great deal of attention in the campus newspaper and in national publications as well (Arnone, 2002a, 2002c; Casselman, 2001; Datta, 2001; Lowe, 2002, February 7; Totty & Grimes, 2001). As the attention increased, Crow became the chief advocate for Fathom with the media and before the University Senate. Crow met frequently with committee members and with other interested faculty and student groups to explain Fathom's operations and how University resources were being used in the company. The immediate outcome of this inquiry was that the money Columbia received from its entrepreneurial activities (e.g., patents and licensing revenue), which Crow controlled, became subject to the University's normal budgetary process, including review by the University Senate.

Crow's role in bridging the gap between Columbia and Fathom was substantial. He argued the value and importance of the company with Columbia's students and faculty and also helped Fathom's management more effectively interact with the University.

Stedman also played something of a mediating role between NYU and NYUonline, but to a much lesser extent than Crow. It was unclear whether NYU's board and administration felt that a true mediator was needed, though. Stedman met quite often with Macomber, at least monthly and sometimes every week, calling him his "Black Sheep Dean." Additionally, in Stedman's regular meetings with NYU's deans he frequently advocated for NYUonline as a company the deans should do business with and tried to persuade them to motivate faculty to work with the company. Rather than playing the role of cultural interpreter for NYUonline's managers, Stedman seemed to be most concerned with the business success of the subsidiary. This was in contrast to Crow, who spent a great deal of time trying to bridge the differences in the two organizations. Surely Stedman's work had its positive benefits; however, following the demise of NYUonline, Macomber lamented that NYU had not been sufficiently prepared to interact with the company and that NYU's top leadership had not done enough to help the company connect with the University's academic personnel. Macomber cited this as one of the main reasons for the company's demise.

Duke CE operated without a mediator in the same sense as Stedman and Crow. Sheppard did not concern himself with the relationship between Duke CE and Fuqua and Lange, the University's provost, did not play this role with the larger University. Douglas Breeden, Fuqua's dean and chair of Duke CE's board, did report regularly to Fuqua's faculty on the company's status and Lange communicated with the executive committee of Duke's board of trustees, yet neither acted as a mediator between the two organizations.

Three reasons for the lack of mediation at Duke seem plausible. First, the creation of Duke CE was discussed extensively with Fuqua's faculty and finally approved by them in a formal vote. This process may have given the company legitimacy, particularly with faculty, that was not enjoyed by Fathom or NYUonline. This legitimacy may have lessened the need for advocacy with Fuqua's faculty like that required at Columbia. Second, Duke University had experience in creating and operating highly visible subsidiary companies, including Duke Management Company, a for-profit company that manages the University's endowment, and the Duke University Health System, a nonprofit subsidiary which includes the Duke Medical Center, two local community hospitals, and a large network of smaller care facilities. Keohane admitted "some real tension in the past around the investment company and in the present around the health system" and commented that her involvement with these two organizations was much greater than with Duke CE. The experience gained in dealing with these two organizations may have helped Duke administrators in operating Duke CE or might have just consumed the interest and energy of those that may have opposed Duke CE's operation and creation. Finally, because the level of cultural understanding between parent and subsidiary was so great, a mediator just wasn't needed. Because Duke CE was created from the Fuqua School, rather than the larger University, as was the case with NYUonline and Fathom, the company's sole constituency, to some degree, was the Fuqua School. And because Fuqua was a business school, the amount of mediation between the School and the business operations of Duke CE was minimal. Fuqua faculty knew business and understood the purpose of Duke CE and most of the subsidiary's managers knew the academic culture of

Fuqua and the broader culture of Duke University; therefore, a mediator was not needed in either case.

Similar to Duke CE, Babson Interactive did not need a mediator in its relationship with Babson College because the company was so intertwined with the College and its culture. With faculty on its board and two faculty governance bodies overseeing the subsidiary's work, all seemed to be well informed of the company's operations and satisfied with its nature. Moore and the other Babson Interactive managers were also well known to the College's faculty and administrators. In fact, Moore seemed to enjoy universal trust and respect. Fetters remarked, "I just have a tremendous respect and trust in him." Bill Lawler, a Babson professor, claimed that Moore was the "consummate" academic administrator and that he was "very savvy in terms of getting things done in an academic environment." Fetters claimed that Moore was perfect in the CEO role because he "understood executive education and understood business people's mindsets." This familiarity with the business and academic environments was seen as crucial to Babson Interactive's success.

Ultimately, a mediator was not needed because there was never a cultural gulf between the parent and subsidiary that had to be spanned. Babson Interactive never left campus and never even created its own website, preferring instead to market itself through the school of executive education and graduate school. Moore and another executive continued to maintain positions in both the College and the subsidiary. In short, the relationship was almost seamless, therefore there was little to mediate.

Research on the role of a mediator in newspaper companies facing disruptive technologies highlighted the importance of this person or small group in managing strategy, securing resources, and solving problems between a subsidiary and its parent organization (Gilbert, 2001; Gilbert & Bower, 2002, May). However, this research made no mention of the need for mediation because of disparate cultural values of a parent and subsidiary organization. Yet, where a mediator was present in these organizations, his greatest role seemed to be that of cultural interpreter or guide. Fathom benefited from Crow's work in this regard, while NYUonline seemingly suffered because of its lack of an effective advocate and cultural mediator. Though solving problems and securing resources was also a large part of Crow's work, he was most valuable in explaining Fathom to Columbia and Columbia to Fathom. This seemed most apparent after Crow left Columbia in July 2002 to assume the presidency of Arizona State University. Amid continued discussion of the place of the subsidiary within the University, approximately six months after Crow left Columbia, Fathom was shut down.

LEADERS AND CULTURE

Leaders set the cultural tone of a new organization. In the subsidiaries, when leaders were from academe, the connection to the parent organization was tighter and the level of cultural misunderstanding between the organizations was diminished. No mediator was needed to span the cultural boundary between the organizations.

Each subsidiary's hiring practices were a signal of the level of cultural congruity with its parent. The assumptions, values, and beliefs of Babson Interactive and Duke CE were largely undifferentiated from those of Babson and Fuqua; therefore, they did not need to look externally for management personnel. However, both NYU and Columbia attempted to manage these subsidiaries by hiring external business talent (for the most part), who would bring to each company more business-oriented goals and values, rather than using internal administrators or individuals more familiar with the academic culture and processes of each parent university. Personnel at Babson and Fuqua better understood both the academic and business worlds than administrators at NYU and Columbia, which better adapted them for the subsidiary's management.

Each CEO's background reflected the hoped for integration of the company with the culture and values of the parent. Macomber, a corporate executive and entrepreneur with no background in academe, was hired to lead a company largely insulated from the culture of the University and structurally placed on the outside. He was the "Black Sheep Dean" and probably due to his lack of familiarity with academic culture, found it difficult to interact with NYU's deans. Both he and his company were isolated from NYU and suffered from the lack of mediation by NYU's central administration. In contrast, Moore was trusted by all and even retained his Babson College deanship. He was viewed as the perfect choice to lead a company that was seen as an extension of the College itself and that in many ways embodied Babson's entrepreneurial ethos. Kirschner, a nontraditional corporate executive, was hired as someone familiar with academe, who could also operate successfully in the corporate world. However, she, along with most of Fathom's personnel, had no familiarity with Columbia, which hindered their interaction with the company. Crow labored to bridge the gap between Columbia and Fathom by acting as a cultural interpreter and aided Fathom's management immensely. At Duke CE, Sheppard was an academic insider and a good fit to lead a company that hoped to redefine itself as a cultural hybrid. Yet he also saw the need to maintain essential ties and a close working relationship with the parent institution. Wanting to gain some separation between subsidiary and parent, Sheppard and the company's personnel created a company culture that, though physically distinct from the University, was still quite integrated.

In contrast to the examples at the start of this chapter, Babson Interactive was a part of Babson College. The company's offices blended nicely with the rest of the campus. In fact, Moore retained his office in the graduate school of business, while the rest of the company's personnel worked in a building just inside the College's main entrance. The company shares the building with other administrative units and could easily go unnoticed amid the regular activities of Babson College. Conversely, NYUonline's offices were located on lower Broadway, several blocks from NYU's campus, in "Silicon Alley" as it was called because of the number of high tech companies in the area. Its office environment was fast paced and hectic, fitting the dot com stereotype. Both employees and the company's website proclaimed the separation of NYUonline from the University. Through its personnel NYUonline isolated itself from NYU, but also never created effective communication and mediation mechanisms to overcome this gulf.

SUMMING UP

The following conclusions can be drawn from the data on personnel and leadership in the for-profit subsidiaries:

- The leaders and founding personnel of each subsidiary had a distinct impact on the subsequent culture and operational characteristics of the subsidiary. In essence, the culture of each subsidiary was a reflection of the backgrounds and experiences of these leaders and of other key personnel.
- Each subsidiary's personnel signaled the level of cultural congruity with its parent institution. The assumptions, values, and beliefs of Babson Interactive and Duke CE were largely undifferentiated from those of Babson and Fuqua; therefore, they did not need to look externally for management personnel. However, both NYU and Columbia staffed their subsidiaries by largely hiring external business talent, who brought more business-oriented goals and values, rather than using internal administrators or individuals familiar with the academic culture and processes of each parent university.
- A mediator was used where the cultural gap between the parent and subsidiary was greatest. Michael Crow filled this role for Columbia and Fathom, acting as a cultural interpreter for the two organizations. Stedman was the key connection between NYU and NYUonline but did not play a mediating role for the two organizations, though this seemed to be greatly needed. Because of the familiarity of Babson Interactive's and Duke CE's

personnel with the culture and norms of their parent institutions, neither needed a mediator in the same way as Fathom and NYUonline.

Chapter Five
Faculty and Curriculum:
The Product and the Process

At NYUonline, Macomber used business vernacular to refer to faculty, calling them NYUonline's "supply chain," which had to be "maintained" for the subsidiary to effectively generate educational products. In contrast, a Babson Interactive manager admitted that the company's work was "all about faculty" and that faculty were "central" to the company's work. Fathom managers were not permitted to contact faculty directly regarding courses without first receiving permission from Michael Crow. Columbia later handled all production of Fathom's courses internally, which resulted, in most instances, in the subsidiary being cut off from direct interaction with Columbia faculty. Duke CE had direct access to Fuqua faculty and even hired some professors who were on leave from the School to work for the company full-time.

As these examples illustrate, each subsidiary differed in its relationship with faculty from its parent institution and its approach in working with and employing these faculty. The connection to faculty was constrained for some subsidiaries and open and fluid for others.

This chapter focuses on the role of faculty in the for-profit subsidiary. First, I consider the traditional values and authority of the professoriate and then present data on the work of faculty in these companies, focusing particularly on the relationship between each subsidiary and its parent's faculty. Though these data suggest that the subsidiaries presented challenges to the traditional faculty role, by considering the nature of the curriculum or product line offered by each company, one can see that faculty still retained supreme authority over all credit-bearing courses, and with this authority, considerable influence. To conclude, I discuss the degree of influence faculty held over the subsidiaries and the potential impact of these companies on the traditional faculty role.

FACULTY CULTURE AND VALUES

Professors are fiercely loyal to their disciplines. Because of this, university faculty are said to occupy "academic tribes," which defend their scholarly "territory" (Clark, 1993, p. 163). Despite these divisions, academic culture also provides a "general identity" (Kuh & Whitt, 1988, p. 76) for faculty which cuts across disciplinary and institutional affiliation (Clark, 1984). This common identity rests on three basic values: (1) the pursuit and dissemination of knowledge as the main purpose of higher education, (2) autonomy in the conduct of academic work, and (3) collegiality (Kuh & Whitt, 1988). "An ideal academic community is a college or university in which the pursuit of learning, academic freedom, and collegiality are strongly held values" (Kuh & Whitt, 1988, p. 76). These values are broadly shared across disciplines and institutional types and deviations are strongly resisted (H. R. Bowen & Schuster, 1986). They are reinforced by institutional structures and practices, such as tenure, peer review, and shared governance.

Though these values cross institutional type, they converge in the upper strata of higher education. "The hard core of academic values in the American professorate is found in the leading research universities and top liberal arts colleges" (Clark, 1993, p. 175). In these institutions, particularly large research universities, faculty hold considerable authority. "To sum the story on authority: at the top of the institutional hierarchy, faculty influence is well and strong. . . . As we descend the hierarchy, however, faculty authority weakens and managerialism increases" (Clark, 1993, p. 170).

Under this authority, faculty assert that "they are the only group authorized to establish and modify academic programs and policies" (Kuh & Whitt, 1988, p. 60). Faculty oversee program quality and also monitor workload, conduct peer review and promotion, and shape the overall curriculum. In these functions, faculty expertise and professionalism (Etzioni, 1964) strengthen the claim to "primary responsibility" over the curriculum (AAUP, 1990). In fulfilling this responsibility, faculty operate under a different ideology and value system than the business world:

> If the corporation rests on the principle of hierarchical authority, the collegium rests on the principle of hieratic authority, on the notion that the professoriate constitutes a priesthood when it comes to matters of academic policy and principle . . . it is the ordained members of the community who make decisions. (Downey, 2000, p. 307)

Stemming from this "formidable and ingrained tradition of faculty authority and self-regulation" (Chait, 2002, p. 77), faculty usually decide what, how, and when to teach, maintaining direct and exclusive control over the content of their courses. This authority often overshadows the central prerogatives of administrators and trustees. Damrosch (1995) observed, "It is remarkable how little influence the administration exerts on the intellectual direction of the typical university . . . basic policy is rarely set from the top" (p. 58–59, as quoted in Chait, 2002, p. 77). The decisions of faculty in curricular matters often result in formal institutional policy, where "boards end up approving, after the fact, the continuing and developing mission that lurches up from below" (Nelson, 1999, p. B4, as quoted in Chait, 2002, p. 78).

Yet, faculty not only create policy, but can also confound and constrain central administrative actions in academic or curricular affairs (Chait, 2002). Thus, they become a "conservative force" in higher education (Kuh & Whitt, 1988, p. 60). They are the keepers of culture and have great influence in maintaining an institution's culture, often using a university's processes and structures to minimize change (Kuh & Whitt, 1988).

Challenging Traditional Roles

Some have argued that "the structure of academic work is changing in response to the emergence of global markets" (Slaughter & Leslie, 1997), and that faculty are "moving away" (p. 179) from traditional values toward market values. Others have expressed concern that faculty involvement in market activities will reduce faculty attention to other aspects of their role, including teaching (Fairweather, 1988). However, the literature on this point is inconclusive (Blumenthal, Gluck, Louis, & Wise, 1986; Philpott, 1994). Many believe that faculty "time devoted to commercial activities reduces the share of time and resources" committed to traditional activities (Slaughter & Leslie, 1997), and that a commercial focus puts many faculty "at odds" with traditional values (p. 137).

Kerr notes that the influence of economic factors within the university has resulted in a paradigm shift in academic life, where faculty members are less committed to an academic community and more to the market (Kerr, 1994). Slaughter (2001) asserts that this shift has helped some professors acquire "a star status that enables them to bargain with a university for salary and perks in the same way that major league sports players bargain for multimillion dollar contracts" (p. 22). These professors then "straddle" both the academic and corporate world, "commingling the values of each" (Slaughter, 2001, p. 22). Croissant (2001) contends that as core academic values intermix with corporate priorities, they lose clarity and become "blurred," and that increasing connections between academia and industry "could mean interference and a loss of autonomy" for institutions and faculty (p. 44). Finally, this could result in an "erosion of core academic values" (Croissant, 2001, p. 44).

In the modern university, faculty actually sit at a crossroads. Though they are the keepers of traditional culture and values, they are also the "linchpin" (Allen & Norling, 1991, p. 99) in a university's efforts to enter corporate markets in a quest for greater "competitiveness" (Bird & Allen, 1989, p. 583). Faculty have the knowledge the university wants to sell. Thus, presumably, they can either repudiate this quest and hold true to traditional values and processes or join in the effort and flex their own entrepreneurial muscles. If they pursue the latter option, instead of a keeper of values, entrepreneurial faculty become "a creator of new values" for the university (Bird & Allen, 1989, p. 595), furthering the paradigm shift Kerr described.

ROLE OF FACULTY IN THE SUBSIDIARIES

The actual role of faculty varied among the subsidiaries, but was most multifaceted in Duke Corporate Education. Faculty, or "academic directors," filled a number of functions within the company. Sitkin, a Fuqua professor on leave with the company, explained:

> We have some academic directors who play primarily administrative roles. We have some academic directors who play a client relationship management role. We have some who play a product development role, which is more like an academic content area leadership role. We have some who just do design and program delivery work. Ultimately as we grow, we may have people who just do design and product development work. . . . These are people who can do research, program design, product design, and delivery, or some combination of those.

The role played by Duke CE's academic directors was substantial and came closest to the multifaceted function faculty fill within a university. They helped design, create, and deliver the courses, performed administrative work in the company and also played a key role with clients/students.

Although faculty at Babson Interactive did not participate as fully in the company's activities as was the case at Duke CE, for specific courses they not only helped produce the courses but taught them as well.

At NYUonline and Fathom, faculty primarily acted as "content experts," providing the design and raw material for online courses to subsidiary personnel who then translated the material to a digital format. Rarely at NYUonline and Fathom did these same faculty participate in course delivery. Thus, the faculty role was unbundled. Faculty provided course content, which might include as little as a syllabus listing course materials and the instructional sequence. At NYUonline, this material was then given to freelance writers who compiled the materials, wrote the course, and provided the technical design for putting the course online. Computer pro-grammers were hired to create the actual online course. The faculty's role was thus reduced to a supplier of raw course content.

Access to Faculty

Though the subsidiaries utilized faculty differently, each company relied on faculty to produce material for its customers. In fact, the parent institution's faculty were central in the quest to "leverage the intellectual assets of the university" or "monetize intellectual property," as the work was termed. Yet, even though the subsidiaries were created to provide an outlet within the institution for entrepreneurial faculty activity, in three of the four cases, the connection between each subsidiary and its parent's faculty was con-strained. Only Duke CE could contact faculty in the Fuqua School directly to arrange the creation and delivery of educational material to the com-pany's clients. Babson Interactive, Fathom and NYUonline employed poli-cies or procedures to limit access to faculty in general and to junior faculty in particular. These limitations were meant to regulate the impact each com-pany could have on the parent's faculty.

Gordon Macomber, NYUonline's CEO, complained that he could pick up the phone and contact a professor at any other university in the country more easily than he could at NYU. According to policy set by NYU's central administration, rather than contact individual faculty directly to discuss cre-ating a course or other type of educational product, NYUonline's managers had to first go to the faculty member's dean. Often a contract would have to be signed with the NYU School before the company was granted permission to speak with individual professors. Due to these restrictions, Macomber felt that NYUonline's "access to faculty was hamstrung."

NYUonline did not even enjoy a preferred position with Schools inter-ested in pursuing online education opportunities. Though NYU's central ad-ministration wanted the University's faculty to work with the subsidiary, according to Macomber, each NYU School was also instructed to view NYUonline just like "any other company that they had to do due diligence on before they established a contractual relationship." This potentially lim-ited any advantage NYUonline had over its competitors who also wanted to contract with NYU's Schools and faculty. Each School was free to choose whether or not to do business with NYUonline. Jeff Tagliabue, NYUonline's director of finance and administration, asserted:

> The Schools are getting to work on their own terms. They are not forced
> to work with us; they set up a business relationship on their own. And I

think it is a healthy approach. It is a more business approach than if NYU's administration said, "Okay, we set this company up, you are going to work with them. And I don't care what they give you money wise, what the revenue sharing is. I don't care what they do; you have to do it with them."

Thus, each NYU School maintained control of the "business relationship" between individual faculty and the subsidiary. NYUonline did not negotiate contracts with NYU's Schools; this was handled through the provost's office, which set the amount of revenue that would be shared between NYUonline, the professor, and the School. Tagliabue commented on this negotiation:

> That is something we don't want to get involved in. We are going to let the University deal with how they split the money up. . . . That is a battle. Of course, we haven't made a lot of money on the courses, so I don't think the real battle has happened yet. That battle is still to come.

The requirement that NYUonline work through each School's dean also put Macomber and other managers in a difficult position. The deans were unsure of their position relative to the subsidiary and were unsettled as to what either an affirmative or negative response to a query from NYUonline meant for them and their School with NYU's central administration. Accordingly, Macomber felt that deans saw him as a "big political problem coming at them."

> Deans would look at this trustee/administration baby and then would have politically based concerns about talking with us. They didn't know what the position of the subsidiary was with the administration and how they should position themselves vis-à-vis the subsidiary.

The limits on NYUonline in relation to the University's faculty created real problems. The political issue with the deans, according to Macomber, "created so much thickness there that you could never get to the point with the deans." Because of the constraint on access, Macomber noted that the company "could not fluidly contract with faculty. . . . There were many faculty we could never get to. We would have loved to have gotten to them and talked about opportunities, but it wasn't possible."

Access to faculty was not limited in the same way for Babson Interactive; however, Tom Moore, Babson Interactive's CEO, was circumscribed in his work with individual faculty. Moore enjoyed a relationship of trust with many of Babson's faculty and knew each professor in the graduate school. Though mandated more by norms of collegiality rather than formal policy, Moore spoke with Michael Fetters, Babson's academic vice president, and then to each professor's division chair before he could complete a contract with an individual professor. This process was quite informal though. Fetters admitted that Moore could go straight to the department chairs and avoid talking with him, but noted that he and Moore would usually "talk first because we know the faculty the best." The reason for this consultation was to avoid overtaxing the already stretched faculty. With the same group of faculty teaching in the undergraduate and graduate programs and in the school of executive education, faculty time was very limited. Stephen Laster, Babson Interactive's chief information officer, remarked that "faculty time is a premium asset" and that a "resource conflict" had developed to some extent between the College and the company over the use of faculty time. In essence, Fetters intervened in this conflict and became a gatekeeper in the use of faculty.

Babson Interactive's access to faculty was also curbed, for "political reasons." As a result, the company was forced to work with several faculty who were not Moore's first choice. He remarked that "There have been issues around who gets to play. Some faculty feel left out that would want to participate. As a result, I've had to swallow a few players in the program, because of political reasons, that I would have chosen not to otherwise."

The politics centered on the relationship between Moore and Fetters. When Fetters asked Moore to use a professor who was not his first choice, Moore felt obligated to honor Fetters's wish, even though Moore worried that the quality of the course would suffer. In one situation, Fetters wanted Moore to use a female accounting professor who did not have experience with online education and was not able to travel, which the work required. According to Moore, "she was not technology savvy and reluctant to put things online, where another member of the group had been an early pioneer in e-learning." However, Fetters advised Moore to work with the female professor and "for political reasons [Moore] acquiesced." Thus, Fetters had substantial control over the faculty whom Babson Interactive employed.

Moore's relationship with faculty was a benefit to Babson Interactive. Just after Babson Interactive's creation, faculty worked for the subsidiary with only a handshake agreement because a contract that was agreeable to both parties had not been produced. Faculty continued to work with the company to produce online material for several months while a satisfactory contract was created. The trust that was needed to perform work in these circumstances was due to Moore's position in the company. When asked why he was chosen as CEO, Moore admitted that he was chosen because they "didn't want to lose direct contact with the sales force—the school of executive education—and with the faculty." He continued, "I think the notion was, how do we create a separate entity to get the benefits of a for-profit, but not lose the leveragability of direct contact with . . . the faculty." This direct contact greatly facilitated the company's interaction with faculty.

Early in its existence, Fathom's "producers," as the company called its personnel who helped develop digital material, worked directly with Columbia's faculty to create the company's online offerings. At that time, access to faculty was limited to certain departments or colleges that were approved to work with the company by Columbia's central administration. This limitation, according to David Wolff, Fathom's vice president of programming and production, came because of overzealous producers who were "cold-calling" faculty to try to convince them to agree to work with Fathom to compose online material. Wolff noted that a short time later, Fathom was told to discontinue contacting faculty directly until the University "had a series of meetings at the higher levels to make sure everybody understands what Fathom is." Following these meetings with certain deans and department heads, Michael Crow, Columbia's executive vice provost, eventually gave Ann Kirschner, Fathom's CEO, and Wolff approval to contact faculty in specific areas of the University. However, Fathom was not allowed to directly contact departments and colleges without Crow's approval.

Later, to limit direct interaction between Fathom personnel and Columbia's faculty and to use internal resources the University had developed to produce digital course material, Columbia committed to develop its own content for Fathom rather than work with the company's producers. Wolff commented that this made his job easier, yet also compounded the difficulty in working with faculty because the company was not able to establish rapport or legitimacy with them directly.

Contact with faculty was unfettered for Duke CE. The company was free to speak directly with faculty in the Fuqua School and also contracted with faculty from other universities. No other subsidiary ventured beyond the parent institution for faculty expertise nor was allowed the autonomy Duke CE had with faculty. When asked if there was a policy limiting the company's access to individual faculty, Bob Reinheimer, an academic director at Duke CE and former Fuqua professor, proclaimed, "There's no policy. We call them directly, as individuals." Blair Sheppard, Duke CE's CEO, remarked that being allowed to work with outside faculty allowed them to "gut Fuqua's competitors" by "tapping the undervalued capacity" of faculty in Fuqua's peer institutions. In this pursuit, Reinheimer noted that Duke CE had contracted with faculty from "at least a dozen institutions" besides Fuqua.

Faculty Terms of Employment

Faculty were employed in various ways by each subsidiary. Both Duke CE and Babson Interactive contracted with faculty for the one-day per week each professor was allowed to spend on consulting work or other outside activities. This gave both companies over 50 days per year of faculty time they could "buy" in order to develop online material. In addition, Duke CE hired individual faculty full-time, most often for one or two years, while they took leave from their tenured positions. When Duke CE was created, seven of Fuqua's faculty joined the company under this arrangement. No other subsidiary employed faculty in this way. Duke CE also created an "academic network" of faculty that the company could call upon in various situations. This network included faculty from varying institutions and disciplines and even former faculty who were working mainly as consultants. Duke CE could either contract with these faculty for specific projects or enter into a longer-term arrangement, whatever was needed. This gave the subsidiary, as Wanda Wallace asserted, "a whole suite of people that you ask, 'Can I call you when I need you?'" According to Wallace, this arrangement gave Duke CE a great deal of flexibility in its work with faculty.

After Columbia determined to produce online course material for Fathom internally, the company's interaction with faculty was reduced significantly. Columbia, in essence, licensed course material for use by Fathom. This arrangement allowed all contracts to be entered directly between the professor and Columbia rather than with Fathom.

After receiving approval, NYUonline arranged with individual faculty for specific projects. The company also contracted with faculty for the one day per week professors were allowed to use for outside consulting, and hired adjunct professors who were affiliated with NYU's School of Continuing and Professional Studies to produce specific courses. These individuals were often consultants or business leaders with expertise in a particular subject as well as experience in creating online educational material (Carr, 2000b). The company also worked with particular NYU Schools to develop curricular products, such as the College of Dentistry, to create online material that was used in continuing professional education courses offered by the College.

CURRICULUM: WHAT IS OUR PRODUCT?

Each of the subsidiaries followed a different approach to delivering educational material. Though Fathom itself did not offer courses for credit, especially those created by Columbia, many of its partner institutions offered credit-bearing courses through the company's website. A central part of Fathom's overall business plan was to become a "portal," where "lifelong learners" could access courses that were guaranteed to meet high quality standards. Fathom promoted this material as "authenticated" or "certified knowledge." In addition to these courses, Fathom offered free on its website the text of roughly 800 lectures and articles. These giveaways were meant to attract a loyal customer base that would then sign up for the longer and more expensive courses offered by the company, which could cost as much as $500 each. Fathom would then receive a royalty on each course it sold.

This approach, however, was not successful. Kirschner commented that the courses were "too expensive" and "too long" (Tedeschi, 2001). Consonant with this philosophy, Fathom began marketing shorter courses that sold for $25 to $50 each. Many of these "short courses" were offered free to Columbia alumni in an effort to interest them in the company's material. In a similar effort to increase revenue, Fathom began offering its products to corporations for use in corporate training (Arnone, 2002b; Carlson, 2001a; Tedeschi, 2001). This material was largely contributed by several for-profit companies Fathom had partnered with to create a "Professional Development Learning Center" as part of its website. Some wondered openly how this move "[meshed] with Fathom's original mission to deliver high-quality academic content" (Arnone, 2002b).

The nature of the product NYUonline delivered evolved as the needs of the market emerged. After withdrawing from the idea of delivering credit-bearing courses to students—the "retail market," as company personnel termed it—NYUonline sought to produce and sell educational material directly to corporations. In this effort, the company began to sell full-length courses that were not much different than traditional college courses offered for credit over the Internet by many universities. However, consistent with Fathom's experience, when demand for these courses lagged because of the amount of time it took for a person to actually complete the course—sometimes as long as nine hours—NYUonline began to disassemble them and produce smaller instructional modules that centered on a particular concept and might only take a person from 25 minutes to an hour to complete. Finney remarked:

> Companies want knowledge in . . . independent bite sized chunks, and taking pieces of knowledge out of context is tricky at best. . . . And I think that their goal is to be able to walk into a company and pull learning modules off the shelf and deliver . . . a custom made educational solution to whatever training problem a company has.

NYUonline executives were convinced that the corporate training market was where the company would find real success and that the potential rewards in this market were significantly larger than those offered by delivering traditional courses to students. Macomber argued:

> Many business models have crashed and burned because e-learning companies have merely developed courses. The corporate market wants granular modules of information. . . . We are developing a repository of un-branded learning objects that customers can customize. This is a business model that makes tremendous sense. (Evans & Previte, 2001)

These "learning objects" were originally marketed to corporate universities, other corporate training programs, and to those interested in meeting state-mandated continuing professional education requirements (Kocijan, 1999). Eliminating credit-bearing courses from the company's repertoire lessened the need for faculty involvement in the final stages of creation, approval, and delivery of online material, thus further removing the company from the operations of its parent.

Because of the non-credit nature of the product, faculty had limited review over the material NYUonline produced. In addition, they played a very limited role in the editing and final production of online content and did not have final approval rights on material used for the company's learning objects. Finney confirmed that faculty had no veto power or ultimate review rights over the quality of the non-credit material NYUonline produced. In discussing this role, Finney remarked:

> It doesn't have to be up to snuff for the faculty member, it has to be up to snuff for the company and whomever they're trying to sell it to.
>
> *So really, quality is consumer driven?*
>
> Yes.

Confirming Finney's statement, Lloyd Short, NYUonline's senior vice president of e-learning, noted that if a customer wanted the online content the company was producing, but the material was still waiting for a professor to review, NYUonline would deliver the material to the customer and just not "brand" it with NYU's name or the name of the individual school, but instead use NYUonline as the sole source. Thus, even though faculty did participate to a limited extent in reviewing the online material produced by NYUonline, the customer served as the final judge of quality.

Duke Corporate Education's business plan focused on delivering "customized" educational programs to corporate clients. Duke CE met client's needs by combining online educational material with in-person seminars, whichever was appropriate for the particular situation. Essentially, this was the same work that most of the company's personnel had performed in the Fuqua School's customized executive education program before it was spun-off as Duke CE. Faculty worked with technical personnel to design and produce the online courses and then also participated in course delivery. Duke CE's team-based work orientation facilitated its efforts to serve individual clients. For each client, a team was formed to design, create, and deliver the educational program, customizing it to meet the client's particular circumstances. Because this work was client specific and highly individualized, no academic credit was given. Thus the company worked solely to meet the training needs of corporations.

The quality of the material Duke CE produced was monitored and controlled by the individual team. No oversight bodies of any kind were created to independently monitor quality. Instead, Sheppard asserted that the quality of the company's materials could be judged by the quality of the clients it served. "High quality clients demand a high quality product," Sheppard remarked, so no curricular oversight was necessary.

Babson Interactive was the sole subsidiary to offer credit-bearing courses. The centerpiece of the company's work was the Intel MBA, a customized master's of business administration program designed exclusively for Intel's managers. This program combined online courses with traditional classroom discussion that took place at the company's workplace. The curriculum was broadly created to meet specific training needs identified by Intel, though it also contained essential courses to meet degree requirements.

For Babson Interactive's credit-bearing courses, two faculty governing bodies were created, a "design committee" and an "oversight committee." The former examined the design of courses and programs as they were developed, while the latter monitored quality as well as faculty workload, the rigor and comparability of courses offered by Babson Interactive, and other faculty issues that might arise. Both governing bodies were sanctioned by and reported to the graduate school's curriculum committee.

For the company's non-credit courses, however, different rules applied. These courses were driven by the demands of the market, where, according to Moore, "the customer [is] the arbiter of quality." Fetters concurred:

> You just do what the client wants. . . . [The faculty] know that we have to move with the market, that the market is the arbitrator of what sells and what doesn't sell, and that if the market is demanding integrated education, we have to deliver that. If they are demanding online education, that's what we have to deliver.

FACULTY INFLUENCE

For the most part, faculty were divorced from any significant governance role in these subsidiaries (Babson Interactive the exception), and had limited control over non-credit courses. However, they still retained substantial influence. A prime example was the inquiry by Columbia University's Senate into Fathom's operations. As discussed in Chapter 4, this began with the formation of a joint subcommittee of the Budget, Education, External Relations, and Student Affairs Committees to address a "number of concerns that individual faculty raised about the University's overall Internet strategy in general, and about Fathom in particular." In March 2001, a formal resolution was adopted by the Senate to establish an ad hoc committee to explore the impact and extent of Columbia's online learning and digital media initiatives. This committee was charged to answer the following questions:

- What is the appropriate balance between the commercial and academic interests of the University?
- What incentives do these new media technologies create for faculty and research staff?
- Can Columbia's brand name for excellence be preserved in the face of commercial pressures? (Senate, 2001)

Both the original joint subcommittee and the ad hoc committee received a great deal of attention from campus and national media. This attention focused on the money that was being invested in Fathom and the University's other digital media initiatives. These funds consisted mainly of patent and license royalties that were controlled by Crow, but that were not included in the University's normal budgetary review process and thus not subject to review by faculty. The initial joint subcommittee was created after the revelation, in 2000, that the University had invested $18.7 million in Fathom and had committed another $10 million over the next two years. Whether it was a direct result of the committee's work is debatable, but at about this same time, Fathom undertook "an internal reorganization." In early 2001, the company dropped its marketing department and focused instead on "[expanding] its offerings to emphasize the creation of high-quality e-courses from Columbia and its member institutions" (Cole, 2001). (See also Carlson, 2001b; Casselman, 2001; Datta, 2001; Lowe, 2002, February 7) The company also shifted its business plan to focus more on the corporate training market and less on selling traditional academic courses.

An increased level of external accountability for the company matched these internal changes. As a result of the inquiry, the Senate was granted full review rights over the patent and licensing revenue controlled by Crow. In addition, a monthly meeting was established between Crow and the Senate committee's chair to review Fathom's operation and prospects for the future.

Though faculty involvement in NYUonline was minimal, they did exert influence through course content. Macomber articulated the role of the faculty:

> The entities that are successful in this business focus on their supply chain. They focus on creating the technology that can engage their supply chain, which is the faculty. If you do that, you have a big thing taken care of. . . . We have really endeavored to be at the leading edge of the educational technology tools that we are offering to NYU. That keeps our supply chain in tact.

According to Macomber, faculty, or the company's "supply chain," were as critical to NYUonline as a logging company is to a paper manufacturer. As suppliers of the raw material needed to manufacture online courses, faculty had influence over the company through the "inputs market" (Blair, 1995, p. 24). Without the participation of NYU faculty in the company, it would not be able to create its products. If faculty refused to supply material to NYUonline, Macomber could recruit faculty from outside NYU; however, this would have defeated one of the purposes of creating the company and also lessened the cachet of NYUonline's products because they would lack the label, "made by an NYU professor." Finney noted that because of faculty control of course content, Macomber had to do whatever was necessary to convince them to work with the company:

> As a matter of practical reality, [Macomber] has got to rely on the institution to provide him with intellectual content. And so he has got to play, at least pretend to play, at the political game of talking to and working with deans to figure out what kinds of benefits might accrue to them, their schools, and their faculties by playing this game.

Even though NYUonline sought to exclude faculty from governance, the traditional academic value of faculty control over the curriculum was powerful. Before the company was shut down, Macomber considered creating an advisory board composed of NYU's deans as well as faculty advisory boards by subject area, to give faculty and deans more influence in the subsidiary, even though it still only produced noncredit-bearing material. Macomber stated that faculty should "feel that they have some power over this company, even if it is only in an advisory role." These advisory boards may have given the deans some minimal level of sway in the governance of the company, but still would not have provided a formal avenue for faculty involvement in governance. Therefore, this might have been merely a symbolic move by Macomber to earn NYUonline greater legitimacy with faculty. However, regardless of intent, the need Macomber felt to create a faculty advisory board underscored the power of the academy's cultural norm of faculty control over the curriculum and involvement in governance in curricular matters.

Managers at Babson Interactive argued that the subsidiary was "all about faculty."

> It's all about faculty commitment. It's all about asking faculty to risk a new delivery model, to move out, way out, of their comfort zones. It isn't about technology or profit.

To educate faculty about the company, Babson Interactive sponsored several workshops, led by Moore, which covered copyright issues, modeled the technology used by Babson Interactive, and discussed the role of faculty in creating and delivering courses. These helped to not only give the company greater legitimacy with the faculty, but also enticed many to participate who may not have otherwise.

Faculty working with Babson Interactive had a great deal of influence because of the company's credit-bearing courses and degree programs. As Allan Cohen, a Babson professor explained, faculty expected influence in the company because of its credit-bearing courses:

> If it were only executive education, faculty would expect to have a voice, but not as much control. However, the minute you have to give degrees, really bizarre stuff comes into play. Because we will do both degree and non-degree programs, faculty expect and demand a much greater degree of control.

Moore acknowledged, "I have a much freer hand where the product is going to the non-credit executive market, than if it's a degree program. . . . Even though we're a for-profit, we still have to satisfy the degree folks."

CHALLENGING FACULTY ROLES

These subsidiaries presented challenges to the traditional role of faculty in the academy. Not only did they present difficult career decisions for junior faculty who often struggle with the desire for more income and the need to use their time productively in the pursuit of tenure, but they also threatened to stratify the faculty world, dividing those who could successfully teach on-line from those who could not. These threats were present in each of the subsidiaries, yet none fully came to fruition.

Threat to Junior Faculty

Richard Bulliet, a Columbia professor and chair of the University Senate's joint subcommittee on Fathom, noted the potential perverse incentive the subsidiary provided for junior faculty who had not yet reached tenure. Bulliet remarked:

> It puts the junior faculty, who are the ones who might be most savvy and cutting edge and amenable to this sort of thing, in a very awkward position. Do they do a job for hire, and augment their income, because it doesn't show up as salary or do they stick to their last and do what in the long run they have to do to get tenure?

Bulliet argued that junior faculty could be distracted from the research and teaching vital to a successful tenure decision by the lucrative opportunities the subsidiary provided. Because the work was "off-load" or not counted in a professor's regular mix of research and teaching, a junior faculty member could "double-dip" as Bulliet termed it, by collecting her normal salary and then collecting a "bonus" by working for the subsidiary. However, because a tenure committee could look at this type of activity as inappropriate or even "unscholarly," time spent creating online material could be detrimental to junior faculty. Fetters concurred, noting that the primary reason he monitored Babson Interactive's use of faculty was to avoid putting junior faculty in a position that would potentially hurt their long-term career development:

> I think it's hard for faculty. You know, Tom can go and say, "I really need you. This is so big for Babson." And somebody that's a year pretenure, would say, "God, Tom Moore is asking me, I'd better do it." So frankly sometimes faculty don't make good decisions. They need money. But at some point someone has to say, "If you keep doing this, you're not going to get tenure. . . . You've got to stop doing things for money because you're not published enough or your teaching is not going as well as it should."

Threat to the Curriculum and Composition of the Faculty

In a similar vein, Bulliet speculated that if Fathom was really successful, the company could begin to alter faculty roles and also influence the curriculum:

> I didn't see how, if this really grew and took off in the way they were hoping, I didn't see how this could avoid changing the mix of faculty activities and expectations. . . . Now the whole idea that we are paid extra for online activities, when we are not paid extra for anything else, singles out the online activities as something that in many people's lives are going to gain a stronger appeal than they would otherwise. It's also going to split the faculty between those who can and those who can't.

If the company enjoyed substantial success, Bulliet worried that Columbia would begin to hire faculty that were very good with online material, but who perhaps were not as strong in the traditional research and teaching role, eventually changing the nature of the faculty. Similarly, if faculty had to choose between creating a course that could be used online versus a traditional high quality course that could only be presented in the traditional classroom, because of the monetary incentive the online course provided, they would always create it first:

> A course that was particularly appealing to off-campus users might make very good sense, from a Fathom point of view, because of the profits that it's generating, even though the course is of little interest to on campus users. However the potential likelihood of a course attracting substantial off-campus attention can be related to simplicity. And if not a dumbing-down, then at least, let us say, a level of clarity that we don't usually have in our classrooms.

Eventually, as Bulliet argued, this could lead to changes in the nature and quality of the curriculum.

These types of concerns seemingly drove the policies and procedures that were meant to limit access to faculty in general and to junior faculty in particular. With the exception of Duke CE, each of the subsidiaries employed similar restrictions as part of an effort to regulate each company's impact on the use of faculty time and resources. However, it was unclear why these types of regulations did not operate at Duke CE. There are at least two possible explanations. First, perhaps because the company was created to reduce the growing divide between research oriented faculty and those more inclined to do the "clinical" work of executive education, Fuqua administrators did not feel the same need to monitor the company's use of faculty as it did before these activities were separated from the School. In essence, the company did not present as great a threat to traditional values when separated from the School. Second, hiring faculty on a full-time basis may have eliminated the potential resource conflict that other institutions experienced when faculty struggled to fulfill their normal responsibilities and work for the subsidiary on the side. By contracting for 100 percent of a professor's time, there were no time conflicts.

Credit versus Non-credit

The difference between faculty involvement in credit-bearing courses as opposed to non-credit courses was stark. Faculty were in a familiar position with credit-bearing courses. They took center stage in the creation, development, and delivery of these courses and also reviewed their content and comparability with similar courses offered by the parent.

In non-credit courses, however, the position of the faculty was very different. Fathom seemed to isolate Columbia's faculty from the company's operations. Similarly, at NYUonline, faculty were removed, as much as possible, from the process of course design, production, and delivery. Alternately, Duke CE used its full-time academic directors to guide and monitor the creation of the company's educational material from beginning to end, keeping the traditional faculty role largely in tact. For Babson Interactive's non-credit courses, the faculty were used to produce the course material but retained limited control over its final use. Thus, for Fathom and NYUonline, faculty became mere "content providers," or a link in the course production "supply chain." At Duke CE, they were central to the production of these courses, however, these faculty were, for the most part, full-time employees of the company, who had developed and supported the company's operational processes. They were not part-time or project based "consultants" as was the case in the other subsidiaries. Even at Duke CE and Babson Interactive, the client was ultimately the final arbiter of quality, rather than the faculty.

In traditional academic governance, credit-bearing courses are the uncontested domain of the faculty. By following this cultural norm and by offering credit-bearing courses and degree granting programs, Babson Interactive kept faculty squarely within its governance structure and operational processes. In non-credit courses they also retained a level of prominence, because of the company's recognition that "it's all about faculty." The situation was related at Duke CE, though there were no formal faculty governing bodies, faculty employed by the company retained oversight of course quality, production, delivery, and evaluation.

Threats to Faculty Autonomy

By restricting subsidiary personnel from contacting faculty directly, Fathom, NYUonline, and Babson Interactive established an administrative "gatekeeper" to faculty. This person was either a dean or department head (or academic vice president in Babson College's case). However it occurred, ultimately, faculty participation in the subsidiary had to be approved by the parent. Shielding faculty, especially junior tenure-track faculty, from the siren song of lucrative work that in the end would not aid their progress towards tenure, and might actually harm it, was a key concern to university officials. In essence, these regulations were meant to protect faculty from making bad choices.

However, this protection also limited each professor's prerogative to decide whether to participate with the company. Though no data indicated that faculty reacted negatively to this administrative control, one could speculate that if the subsidiaries had experienced significant financial success, thereby providing substantial income to participating faculty, many faculty who were being "protected" from working with the companies would have likely protested these arrangements. Paradoxically, although faculty retained influence, they lost autonomy, with administrators gaining a measure of control over an individual professor's ability to choose whether or not to work for the subsidiary. Thus, the often delicate equilibrium between administrators and faculty could be affected, with administrators becoming gatekeepers to faculty opportunity.

Greater control by administrators may lead to more university activities being pushed to the periphery of the university as they seek greater discretion in their work. "Academic capitalism presses for decentralization of power to the operating units" (Slaughter & Leslie, 1997). Thus, the core of the university shifts to an "entrepreneurial periphery" (p. 208). This periphery is then controlled by administrators to a greater extent and further removed from faculty oversight.

Power of the Market

The for-profit subsidiary, a market-driven piece of the university, presented an unfamiliar challenge and problem to faculty. Members of the joint subcommittee who originally investigated the operations of Fathom were aware that a critical final report by the committee could have significant ramifications for Fathom with potential investors which the company was courting at the time. Bulliet, the subcommittee's chair, realized the report would be picked up by the media because of the intense interest in the company and in the subcommittee's work. In the end, however, he noted that the report was written without considering its possible market ramifications.

Academic freedom and tenure provide a professor license to criticize the institution in general and the operation of the subsidiary in particular; however in the case of a for-profit subsidiary, this criticism might induce a negative response from the capital market by lessening investor confidence in the company's future prospects. This poses a new dilemma and challenge for faculty. As Bulliet asserted, "The bottom-line is not the line they are expected to look at." Faculty who do monitor the bottom line, however, might feel their freedom to criticize the subsidiary or even the parent institution was limited because of possible negative market reaction.

SUMMING UP

The following conclusions can be drawn from the data on the role of faculty in the work of these subsidiaries.

- In many ways, these subsidiaries challenged the traditional faculty role. The use of faculty by the companies often created conflicts over faculty time and loyalty. Policies at Babson College, NYU, and Columbia limited faculty autonomy to choose their own work because the parent institution was the go-between. Administrators essentially took the decision of whether to work with the company out of faculty hands by restricting the subsidiary's access to faculty, thus limiting faculty autonomy and increasing administrative control. Only Duke CE and the Fuqua School left these decisions entirely to the individual professor.

- Faculty retained authority over credit-bearing courses. NYUonline and Duke CE did not produce credit-bearing courses at all in order to avoid faculty oversight in this area. Fathom did offer credit-bearing courses that were produced by its partner institutions, but none from Columbia University. In offering these courses, Fathom acted solely as a distributor. Babson Interactive did offer credit-bearing courses and created two faculty governing bodies to monitor the content and quality of these courses and related faculty issues.

- Access to faculty was another indicator of the degree of cultural congruity, or "fit," between parent and subsidiary. With administrators wary of any direct interaction between the subsidiary and faculty, NYUonline and Fathom were essentially quarantined from their parents. This reduced the odds of "infection" or "cultural contamination." Though there were no formal restrictions, faculty use by Babson Interactive was monitored closely. In contrast, at Duke CE, faculty were fully integrated. The company interacted and accessed faculty with an ease the other subsidiaries could not match. Faculty were a vital part of Duke CE's business and treated as such.

- Regardless of the degree of separation between faculty and the subsidiary, faculty enjoyed substantial influence over the subsidiaries, both formally and informally. The culture of curricular control over for-credit courses by the parent institution was so strong that the subsidiaries could not circumvent it. Even when faculty were largely removed from governance and excluded from a meaningful oversight role in the curriculum, they eventually attempted to rebalance the governance scales in their favor. This was seen most vividly at Fathom in the actions of the University Senate. Faculty became involved in the company regardless of what administrators and managers wanted or hoped.

Chapter Six
Integrated or Insulated: Cultural Fit in the Academy

The central purpose of my research was to determine how for-profit subsidiaries, which were established to deliver online education, were governed in relation to their nonprofit university parents. Because many of the key concerns about for-profit subsidiaries in higher education center on values and beliefs, I used organizational culture as the theoretical lens to view the subsidiaries. I wanted to determine why each parent institution created a for-profit subsidiary, how the governance of these companies occurred in practice, and how the governance structures and processes of the subsidiary reflected or diverged from the culture and values of the nonprofit parent. Finally, I sought to explore and determine the effects of congruence or divergence between the parent and the subsidiary.

The fit varied greatly. Babson Interactive remained on campus, was managed by a Babson College dean, and designated a seat for faculty on its board of directors. NYUonline moved to Broadway's "Silicon Alley," and hired several corporate executives as key managers, who could not, however, speak to NYU faculty without prior approval from a University administrator. Fathom maintained an Academic Council of academic administrators from member institutions and worked effectively with Columbia's alumni office, but was mostly insulated from contact with Columbia faculty in the course production process. Duke CE was managed largely by former Fuqua School administrators, hired many faculty to work for the company on a full-time basis, and had unfettered access to Fuqua faculty.

These examples indicate the range of congruence between the subsidiaries and their parents. At one end of the spectrum, Babson Interactive had numerous connections to its parent. At the other end, NYUonline was largely divorced from the University. Fathom and Duke CE were in between.

This chapter explores several key implications of divergence or congruity between parent and subsidiary. I begin with a summary of the book's major findings, and close by discussing avenues for future research.

GOVERNANCE AND CULTURE

Governance is a reflection of culture. Organizational values and beliefs are manifest in governance structures (Chaffee & Tierney, 1988; Masland, 1991; Schein, 1992; Tierney, 1991). As a controlling and normative force, organizational culture, and particularly academic culture, had a profound effect on these subsidiaries. In the case of NYU and NYUonline, there was intra-institutional incongruity, so there was a greater degree of structural separation between parent and subsidiary and more "foreign" governance arrangements in the subsidiary. Without a separation of the subsidiary from the parent institution, both entities ran the risk that either the traditional academic governance model would be imposed on the subsidiary or that the subsidiary's "corporate" style would infect the University. Especially with respect to access to faculty, the academic community had to be assured that the company was, in effect, quarantined, to minimize the risk of "contamination." NYUonline thus became a contained experiment with governance structures designed to provide a thicker membrane between the parent and the subsidiary because the host institution viewed the subsidiary as very different. To a lesser extent, Fathom followed this same pattern.

At Babson College and Duke's Fuqua School of Business, the subsidiaries were close, next-of-kin to the parents culturally, so there was no danger of contagion, less need for distance, and subsequently more similarity in governance between parent and subsidiary. The traditional academic culture and processes would not contaminate the subsidiaries and the subsidiaries would hardly contaminate the parent because they shared common values and beliefs.

Though each subsidiary was created as the single solution to a set of complex financial, competitive, and organizational problems, a key reason for establishing the subsidiary was to separate the company from the cumbersome governance structures and ponderous decision-making processes of its parent. However, complete separation was never achieved; in essence, each subsidiary was a governance hybrid, with aspects of both the corporate sector and the academy. The degree of similarity in governance reflected the cultural compatibility between the parent and subsidiary which, in turn, derived from a judgment by administrators of the parent and the subsidiary about the risk of cultural conflict between the subsidiary and parent. The governance structures and processes were a byproduct of this calculation.

Though these companies, to some extent, were all hybrids, a finer distinction can be made. Babson Interactive was a cultural purebred, entirely consistent with the values and beliefs of Babson College, while NYUonline was very nearly corporate in spirit and in form. In contrast, Fathom was a true hybrid, with elements of both nonprofit and for-profit governance, but structurally distinct from its parent institution. Duke CE, though not a purebred like Babson Interactive, exhibited a much greater degree of academic culture than either Fathom or NYUonline.

CULTURAL CONGRUITY AND ECONOMIC VIABILITY

Each subsidiary was created under the assumption that separation from the structures and processes of the parent university would increase the company's economic viability and greatly improve chances for success. This strategy was pursued to different degrees by each institution. Babson Interactive was legally separated from Babson College but, in reality, was still carefully integrated into the processes, structures, and values of the College. In contrast, NYUonline was insulated from NYU and interaction between the two entities was carefully monitored and controlled.

The degree of divergence from the parent culture had a profound effect on and important consequences for the subsidiaries. When viewed through the lens of organizational culture, the potential difficulties encountered in bringing the for-profit company into the nonprofit university become clearer. These difficulties are reflected vividly in the lifespan of each subsidiary. Fathom and NYUonline closed after several years of operation and considerable investments. In October 2001, Duke Corporate Education laid off 10 of 77 employees (Mangan, 2001).

For Fathom and NYUonline, closure was attributed to economic conditions, but their failure may, in fact, have resulted from a mismatch between the for-profit, corporate culture of the subsidiary and the traditional academic culture of the parent university (Carlson & Carnevale, 2001). In particular, one commentator argued that the for-profit subsidiary and nonprofit university "seem to be impossible combinations" because of the "fundamental difference in culture" between the two organizations (Wilson, 2003, p. 7). Thus, the demise of these companies may have been caused more by problems of culture rather than problems of capital—a consequence of fit not finances.

The cultural fit continuum, introduced in chapter 3 and reproduced below (see Figure 6–1), is instructive. The two institutions with the least congruity, NYUonline and Fathom, closed. Furthermore, NYUonline, which most diverged from its parent's culture, was the first to shut down. In the

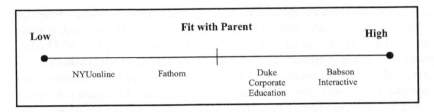

Figure 6–1. Cultural Fit Continuum

case of the other two subsidiaries, Duke CE, though struggling somewhat, continued to predict profitability. Babson Interactive did not exhibit any outward signs of organizational difficulty. These outcomes imply a systematic association between cultural congruity and the economic viability of these institutions. Though a causal relationship cannot be established, these data indicate that the viability of for-profit subsidiaries relates to the degree of compatibility between the cultures of the parent and subsidiary. At the very least, congruity contributed to longevity for the subsidiaries.

Because culture defines the limits of appropriate behavior in an organization, whether a subsidiary's structures, processes, values, and even personnel align with the parent culture is crucial. Birnbaum (1988) asserted:

> Organizational cultures establish the boundaries within which various behaviors and processes take place. By helping to create shared symbols, myths, and perceptions of reality, they allow participants to make sense of an equivocal world and to establish a consensus on appropriate behavior. (p. 80)

The cultural gap between each parent and its subsidiary varied. NYU did not want NYUonline too close to its operations, as if the company would weaken or attack cultural norms, or be rejected by the "host organ." Stedman remarked that NYUonline needed a "separation from the historical protocols of the [University], so that it could make its own way with less of the entanglement of the place." Finney noted, "In terms of the divergent cultures, yes, I think it is important to keep the company at arm's length, and that is why it is structured the way it is." Similarly, Fathom was to "have an arm's length relationship" with Columbia. This was accomplished, according to Sharyn O'Halloran, a Columbia professor who chaired the University Senate's ad hoc committee on digital media, by "insulating" the subsidiary from the culture and operations of the University. This insulation would allow Fathom to "forge ahead" and "prosper."

However, it seemed that for Fathom and NYUonline, insulation from the parent organization engendered more problems than prosperity. The barriers to faculty hindered product development. Managers of both subsidiaries were uneasy with the parent institution's culture and with academic culture more generally. As a result, interaction between parent and subsidiary was stifled.

It was critical to NYUonline's managers that the company operate more like a business rather than a university. Tagliabue remarked that he and Macomber were managing NYUonline, "like we would any company." Macomber agreed, "We are running in the classic business style and to some degree it has to be run that way." In the effort to be a business, they rejected all aspects of the academy that may have helped the company better relate to NYU faculty. More importantly, managers at both NYUonline and Fathom did not enjoy the level of trust from the parent that was needed to forge productive relationships with individual professors, deans, and other university personnel. The buffer between the parent and subsidiary created barriers that could not be overcome. In the end, "arm's length" became an insurmountable distance between the two organizations.

In contrast, Moore claimed that Babson Interactive should not "lose contact" with the College's faculty or the school of executive education and argued that "direct contact" with the faculty was a key to the company's success. He felt that "operating at arm's length" would seriously impede the company. In fact, Moore admitted that his goal was to "integrate Babson Interactive" with Babson College.

Duke Corporate Education was already integrated, through its personnel, with the Fuqua School. Separation from the culture of Fuqua or Duke was never intended. Indeed, to guard against that possibility, most of the company's top executives were, quite deliberately, selected from among the ranks of Fuqua faculty or administrators. All original employees were formerly at Fuqua, and at least seven Fuqua professors were hired by the company on a full-time basis. These faculty became "academic directors" with considerable influence in the company. Though operating under a different name and in a different location, Duke Corporate Education was almost an extension of Fuqua. The company did, however, become a "cultural hybrid" by incorporating aspects of corporate culture into its operations and by eliminating the perceived drawbacks of academic culture. Yet, in the end, integration was never in doubt. Many Duke CE employees were paid through the University in order to retain retirement benefits and employee seniority, and when Duke CE had to lay off workers, most once again became Duke University employees. This was not the case when Fathom and NYUonline were closed.

Perhaps the greatest evidence of integration was that Babson faculty who produced course material for Babson Interactive were "doing it on good faith." Moore noted that for nearly a year, formal contracts with faculty "had been hand shakes;" early on, no professor had a formal employment contract with the company. This relationship paralleled collegial governance. Babson Interactive was an almost seamlessly integrated extension of the College's structure and culture. Babson Interactive was just what a person familiar with the College would expect, a company with the same values and operating style as the parent organization. For-profit companies and entrepreneurial activity are the business, not the bane, of Babson College.

Congruence between structures and values matters. An organization is acting according to "collectively valued purposes in a proper and adequate manner" (Meyer & Rowan, 1977, p. 346) when its structures match the values of the prevailing culture. In this sense, "organizations structurally reflect socially constructed reality" (p. 346). Chaffee and Tierney (1988) contend that for an institution to reach a state of equilibrium, its structure and values must be congruent. A mismatch can cause "structural and normative contradictions within the culture" (p. 28). This is often the case, as officials try to align their institution's internal structure with external demands or opportunities. Without alignment, tensions result and these "contradicting valences can create serious problems in the long run" (Chaffee & Tierney, 1988, p. 183).

When structures and values are aligned, however, a new organizational structure or, in this case, a subsidiary, "becomes legitimate" (Meyer & Rowan, 1977, p. 349). With legitimacy a subsidiary organization can solidify support and improve chances for survival.

> Organizations must have the confidence of their environments, not simply be in rational exchange with them. And those that have this confidence and legitimacy receive all sorts of social resources that provide for success and stability. (Meyer & Rowan, 1978, p. 107)

Organizations that do not incorporate culturally acceptable elements of structure lack legitimacy and become "more vulnerable to claims that they are . . . unnecessary" (Meyer & Rowan, 1977, p. 350), or even potentially dangerous to the parent organization. Thus, the success of for-profit subsidiaries may depend as much on legitimacy derived from congruency between structures and values as on financial and market considerations.

The quest for legitimacy was an important pursuit of the subsidiaries from the outset. Attempts by university administrators and subsidiary managers to "rewrite" (Kanter, 1983, p. 284) or "reinterpret" (p. 412) the parent's institutional history in order to demonstrate cultural congruence with the subsidiary blurred the subsidiary's real purpose. This ambiguity of purpose helped provide legitimacy for each company, particularly for Fathom and NYUonline, within each parent's broad goals. Most of these messages, aimed at faculty, stressed that the company was consistent with the institution's history, mission, beliefs, and values. These messages were essential for the new company to be accepted by its parent organization.

Efforts to gain legitimacy became an enduring struggle, particularly for Fathom and NYUonline. The isolation of Fathom and NYUonline from their parent universities undermined attempts to gain legitimacy, particularly with faculty. Without legitimacy, "resources," both cultural and financial, were harder to acquire and retain.

Legitimacy for each company depended on the faculty. Without a direct tie to faculty, NYUonline and Fathom struggled to gain legitimacy. NYU faculty eyed NYUonline and its managers warily, and often from afar, because the University circumscribed the company's interactions with faculty. A lack of legitimacy for Fathom prompted Columbia's senate to challenge Fathom's operations and existence, which resulted in the eventual loss of crucial financial resources.

Lack of legitimacy and congruity was a "cost" to NYUonline and Fathom, who paid dearly for their lack of legitimacy with faculty and cultural incongruity. Without cultural congruity and internal legitimacy, the for-profit subsidiary and nonprofit university may be an "impossible combination" (Wilson, 2003, p. 7).

THE TIES THAT BIND: FACULTY AND CULTURE IN THE LOOSELY COUPLED SYSTEM

Each subsidiary had an "experimental" quality. Fetters and Moore both spoke of Babson Interactive as an "experiment" in a time of technological change. Similarly, Rupp and Crow at Columbia and Stedman and Finney at NYU both noted the experimental nature of their subsidiaries. As experiments, these subsidiaries reinforced Weick's (1976; 1990) notion of universities and colleges as "loosely coupled systems," where organizational elements are "responsive, but retain evidence of separateness and identity" (Weick, 1976, p. 3) and where elements affect each other "suddenly (rather than continuously), occasionally (rather than constantly), negligibly (rather than significantly), indirectly (rather than directly), and eventually (rather than immediately)" (Weick, 1982, p. 380).

Weick (1976) asserts that loosely coupled systems are optimal for experimentation, or "localized adaptation" (p. 6), where changes can be made to one part of the system without effect on the whole. However, "this same loose coupling can also forestall the spread of advantageous mutations" through an organization (p. 7). Thus, the for-profit subsidiary can be created as an experimental response to external stimuli, but the very nature of the university discourages the integration of the company and cross-fertilization between the company and the university.

An adaptation, or experiment, deemed dangerous to the loosely coupled system as a whole, can be quickly and naturally quarantined, preventing system-wide change (Weick, 1976). The for-profit subsidiary that is not culturally congruent with its parent can be effectively isolated from the rest of the university. Thus, without compatibility, integration becomes nearly impossible. The resulting isolation protects the parent, but dooms the subsidiary. The university, while an "exquisite mechanism" (Weick, 1976, p. 7) for experimentation, is poorly suited to comprehensive or systemic long-term change as a result of isolated experiments.

Culture can be crucial to this dialectic between experimentation and continuity. Because loose coupling inherently "carries connotations of impermanence, dissolvability, and tacitness" (Weick, 1976), some centripetal force must operate to hold the organization together. In the university, culture serves this purpose and functions as the "glue" (Tushman & O'Reilly, 1996, p. 21; Weick & Orton, 1990, p. 212) or cohesive force (Meyer & Rowan, 1977). The carriers of the culture are faculty members, who work to perpetuate a university's beliefs and values (Kuh & Whitt, 1988). In operational terms, the faculty were the key cultural connection between each for-profit subsidiary and parent. This conforms to Weick's (1976) assertion that a loosely coupled organization's "technical core" is one of the most common "coupling mechanisms" (p. 4). A university's technical core is its faculty.

Faculty were crucial to the success of these subsidiaries because they created the products that were marketed by the companies. As Macomber of NYUonline correctly observed, faculty were the critical link in the company's "supply chain." Without faculty expertise, the company could not compete in the marketplace. Yet, NYUonline and Fathom "product managers" were isolated from their "suppliers." Because each subsidiary's business centered on leveraging the university's prestige and reputation for quality, and more particularly, the faculty's knowledge and expertise to produce educational material, the greater the degree of separation, the more imperiled the business model. To produce online courses these companies had to engage faculty and accommodate the pace and rhythm of the university. A complete separation might assure freedom from the parent's governance processes; at the same time, separation would severely limit the company's capacity to take products to the marketplace, where the demand was for a product that only faculty could produce, no matter how loosely coupled to the parent organizationally.

The faculty are, of course, critical to any university's success. Yet, as culture bearers they can impede necessary adaptation. Likewise, successful business organizations often have strong cultures with deeply ingrained norms and values that are, at once, a "critical component" of the organization's success and an obstacle to innovation and change (Tushman & O'Reilly, 1996, p. 16). A culture of stability and consistency impedes behaviors that allow risk and ambiguity. As a result, the business literature strongly counsels managers to create subsidiary organizations in order to deal with "disruptive technologies" that may threaten an organization's core product or when the operation of the subsidiary clashes with the parent organization's values or processes (Christensen, 1997; Christensen & Overdorf, 2000; Gilbert, 2001; Gilbert & Bower, 2002, May; Tushman et al., 1997; Tushman & O'Reilly, 1999). In essence, they advise pursuing a loose coupling strategy to avoid culture's centripetal force. With separation, these organizations are then free to operate in a new business environment and context and avoid the "work processes and decision-making patterns that may be dysfunctional in the new environment" (Gilbert & Bower, 2002, May). The distance gives the subsidiary organization the ability to "develop within it the new processes and values required" (Christensen & Overdorf, 2000, p. 73) to take advantage of new market opportunities.

A similar set of prescriptions advises managers who face rapid technological change to create new entrepreneurial units, which allow parent organizations to "operate in multiple modes simultaneously" (Tushman & O'Reilly, 1999, p. 20). These "ambidextrous organizations" (Tushman & O'Reilly, 1996) host "multiple, internally inconsistent architectures, competencies and cultures" (Tushman & O'Reilly, 1999, p. 20), and concurrently nurture efficiency and consistency in the parent organization and improvisation and risk in the new unit. This organizational configuration purportedly helps sustain competitive advantage.

Because of the academic subsidiary's dependence on faculty, however, separation cannot be achieved. Separating the subsidiary from the faculty, and the university's culture, proved to be dysfunctional. The subsidiary's dependence on faculty actually suggests the need for *tight,* not loose, coupling. Hence, Babson Interactive's close connection to its parent is a model.

Similarly, the key to success in the ambidextrous organization is the ability to establish a culture separate and distinct from the parent; in essence, to create cultural loose coupling. Tushman and O'Reilly (1996) cite Hewlett-Packard as an example. While one business unit relies on a stable, conservative culture to produce a line of printers, another segment of the company creates a risk-prone, entrepreneurial culture to develop new products for emerging markets. The new unit's success rests on the ability to differentiate itself from the parent's culture. Notwithstanding these two very different cultures, each springs from shared core values—profitability, utility, and consumerism—and pursue the same ultimate goal. These common threads tie the two cultures together.

This is not the case for universities and for-profit subsidiaries. In universities, rather than providing a common underlying thread that binds the two organizations, culture becomes a source of conflict and alienation. The nonprofit wants to maximize prestige, even at the cost of profitability, while the for-profit subsidiary wants to maximize profit, perhaps even at the cost of prestige. Whereas a corporate culture shared between two companies "provides consistency and promotes trust and predictability" (Tushman & O'Reilly, 1996, p. 23), the potential cultural disparity between the for-profit subsidiary and the nonprofit university parent breeds suspicion and unpredictability. Without congruency between the subsidiary and parent, (preferably through the faculty), culture becomes a divider not a unifier.

The for-profit subsidiary of a nonprofit university requires different governance and management mechanisms than a subsidiary of a for-profit corporation. The corporation can create an isolated culture; if the subsidiary proves profitable, there will be dispersion and continuity. However, even if a university's for-profit subsidiary generates profits, there may be no dispersion or continuity because the university does not necessarily see profitability as a valued outcome.

Loose coupling, though suited for experimentation, creates difficulties for the long-term survival of for-profit subsidiaries. This outcome creates an interesting paradox: the subsidiaries were designed to be largely independent of the university, the academic culture, and faculty governance, in order to increase economic viability; however, the subsidiaries with the most separation were the least viable. In effect, the less culturally recognizable the subsidiary was to the parent, the less likely the organization would survive. This does not conform with the ambidextrous organization or literature on disruptive technologies, where the opposite is true. The goal is to create a unit culturally foreign and unrecognizable to the parent. In the university, however, an alien academic subsidiary will be isolated and rejected.

IMPLICATIONS FOR PRACTICE

These findings have implications for trustees, administrators, and faculty on campuses that are considering or have already created a for-profit subsidiary to market and deliver higher education.

Culture Matters

The clearest implication for practice concerns the importance and power of organizational culture. Despite literature that exhorts leaders to pay attention to culture (Chaffee & Tierney, 1988; Davis, 1984; Deal & Kennedy, 1982; Kotter & Heskett, 1992; Kuh & Whitt, 1988; Masland, 1991; Peters & Waterman, 1982; Schein, 1992, 1999; Tierney, 1991, 1999), academic administrators and managers of for-profit subsidiaries neglected culture. Tierney (1999) asserts:

> Decision-makers usually move structures around, discuss personnel, and draw up a battle plan or "strategy," and, as they head out the door, they point out that they need to massage the culture to make this happen. . . . Culture is the stepchild of decision-making; individuals work on it when they have time. (p. 154)

Paying more careful attention to culture in the governance and management of for-profit subsidiaries may yield important dividends and avert nettlesome problems. Culture must be considered in the subsidiary's design and not merely as a managerial afterthought. As important as competitive strategy may be, how the subsidiary fits with the parent organization may be more significant. A plan centered on dollar signs may seem anomalous to higher education institutions that thrive on shared values, and in the end, may hinder the subsidiary. However, not only the subsidiary's strategy, but the entirety of culture, must be thoughtfully considered. The values, assumptions, and beliefs of parent and subsidiary must be assessed and harmonized to the fullest extent possible. Following this assessment, the subsidiary needs to be positioned and rationalized in a way that makes sense to the parent culture. This may not be possible in all academic institutions. The prospects for success seem far brighter where the subsidiary is an outgrowth of the parent culture and not an escape hatch.

Integration and Insulation

Because of the power of academic culture and the fundamental dependence on faculty in the "supply chain," leaders should work to create meaningful points of connection between the subsidiary and parent—to integrate rather than insulate. Insulation breeds suspicion and opposition; while integration allows the parent culture to take root and ultimately legitimate the subsidiary.

In practical terms, given a choice of whether to create the subsidiary as a unit closely connected to a university's central administration and board of trustees or as a spin-off from the business school, leaders should recognize the clear cultural benefit of a link to a business school or other academic unit whose culture and values are more compatible with a subsidiary whose goal is profitability. Though Columbia and Duke are both prestigious research institutions, because Duke CE emerged from the School of Business, it looked different from Fathom and each company had a very different fate. Duke CE's natural alignment with Fuqua's goals and values, and reliance on academic administrators not outside managers, provided a strong foundation that Fathom lacked. Babson Interactive was not created from a graduate business school but, then, Babson College *is* a business school.

Nurturing connections that allow cultural crossover between parent and subsidiary reaps significant benefits. Rather than retard the work of the company, close connections enhance the subsidiary's legitimacy. Without that credibility, subsidiaries are severely handicapped.

Faculty Give Legitimacy

Some speculate that a for-profit subsidiary devoted to non-credit education for corporations, as opposed to for-credit courses for matriculated students, will reduce cultural conflict (Bok, 2002). The experiences of these subsidiaries challenge that assertion. Whether intended for a corporate audience or for traditional students, courses cannot be created without faculty. Faculty have to generate the product, just as doctors have to do the surgery, or musicians have to play the symphony. This necessitates not only contact with the academic culture, but adherence to dominant norms. Faculty are not only the "keepers of culture" but also the "keepers of credits." They create the educational product and the academic standards by which that product is judged. Theoretically, the faculty would not permit highly profitable, but substandard products to reach the market even if the products met the customers' "needs," but failed to meet the faculty's definition of what one needs to know, especially to earn credit.

That said, the distinction between credit-bearing and non-credit-bearing courses represented a clear line of demarcation. Only Babson Interactive crossed this line to produce credit-bearing courses; others offered only non-credit programs. This strategy was not dictated entirely by markets, but also, by efforts to reduce faculty influence. Babson Interactive, however, did not eschew a close relationship with faculty who had significant oversight of the company through course development and approval.

Following Babson Interactive's approach may be a productive means of building legitimacy and increasing connection. Rather than shunning credit-bearing courses, for-profit subsidiaries should deliver some credit-bearing material, no matter how small, precisely to create closer ties to the faculty. Though Duke CE, Fathom, and NYUonline seemingly gained more flexibility by offering only non-credit materials, what was gained in flexibility may have been lost in linkages and legitimacy. The faculty's relative indifference toward non-credit activity should not be construed as confidence in management.

Internal and External Legitimacy

Each subsidiary needed to have a degree of internal legitimacy to be successful, which derived from faculty and embrace of academic culture. At the same time, there was a need for external legitimacy in the eyes of customers and corporate clients, which had to be achieved, in part, by embrace of corporate culture. In essence, for-profit clients needed to see a corporate education organization, and the nonprofit parent university needed to see a values-based academic institution.

Theorists assert that organizations are driven to isomorphism, that they will change to resemble other organizations with the same set of environmental circumstances (DiMaggio & Powell, 1991). The legitimacy that comes from isomorphism is particularly crucial from a resource dependency perspective (Pfeffer & Salancik, 1978; Slaughter & Leslie, 1997). When one organization relies on another for needed resources, it will increasingly come to resemble its benefactor. For the subsidiaries, this isomorphism worked two ways.

Each subsidiary's need for dual legitimacy created an inherent conflict and contradiction, particularly where the collegial and customer cultures were most at variance. This dilemma resembles the for-profit hospital that must concurrently convince shareholders of its corporate validity and persuade patients and families that the hospital is hardly a corporation, but rather an entity driven by compassion and concern for quality care at any cost. Duke CE seemed to have found the right balance for both environments. To Fuqua, the subsidiary looked like Fuqua, yet to the corporate world it looked very much like a company. Both internally and externally, the company appeared as it should.

University administrators and subsidiary managers alike must be aware of these tensions and craft a company that has both internal and external legitimacy. As Duke CE showed, this requires a careful blend of academic and corporate personnel, obeisance to certain academic values, and a concern for clients' demands, efficiency, and profitability.

People are Culture Bearers

Business literature advocates that subsidiary companies be staffed with a "heavyweight team" (Christensen & Overdorf, 2000, p. 75)—people who bring "outside perspectives" (Gilbert, 2001, p. 292) to the new organization, free from the ingrained assumptions and values of the core business. These outside managers "allow the project to be governed by different values" than the parent organization and are given autonomy and authority "so that new processes and new ways of working together can emerge" (Christensen & Overdorf, 2000, p. 75).

This is difficult and imprudent advice for academic organizations. At NYUonline and Fathom, hiring a "heavyweight" management team accentuated the differences between the corporate and academic cultures. Unfamiliar with academic culture, these outside managers were puzzled by the university's "way of doing things." In the end, these managers were foreign tissue rejected by the host organism or, at least, like American executives abroad unable to adapt to the operative norms of a foreign culture.

Perhaps, academic administrators may be more adept than career business executives at managing a university's for-profit subsidiaries. Experienced academic administrators "speak the language" of the academy, know the culture, and have credibility with faculty. Unlike the argument of the business literature, the "natives," not the newcomers, are better positioned to move between academe and business.

If, however, business executives are chosen to manage a subsidiary, the task of integration between the for-profit subsidiary and nonprofit university may rest with a mediator. This "active integrator" (Gilbert, 2001, p. 291) must work to "protect and legitimize" (Tushman & O'Reilly, 1999, p. 21) the subsidiary and, more importantly, to bridge cultural differences between the parent and subsidiary. Michael Crow performed this function for Fathom and Columbia. Kirshner commented that Crow "[decoded] Columbia" for her (Blumenstyk, 2001, p. A29) and helped her in "waters [she] didn't know how to navigate." He was the main interface between Fathom and Columbia. This may have been so crucial to Fathom's relationship with Columbia, that shortly after he left the University, Fathom was shut down.

No one played the mediator role effectively for NYUonline, a gap that Macomber cited as a reason the company closed. Duke CE and Babson Interactive did not need integrators because the fit was much tighter. Both company's CEOs were products of the parent organization's culture and values. They facilitated effective communication and interaction. There was no foreign tissue to reject because the gene pool was the same as the parent organism.

Business in the Academy

Fathom and NYUonline point to a central lesson for the management and governance of universities. The very ability to close these subsidiaries, lay off personnel, and cease operations sharply illustrates how business-like universities can be (and ultimately how detached the subsidiaries may be from the faculty's concerns). Unlike the typical academic program, these programs were closed with little resistance or controversy. There were no tortured deliberations by academic committees, no tenured faculty to relocate, and no student protests to endure. The decision was made and implemented.

NYUonline and Fathom, demonstrated that even in the academy, you make money, lose money, and move on. Universities are quite familiar with the first two, but have never been able to move on very easily. The fate of these subsidiaries provided concrete evidence that the academy can do business like a business. Alert presidents and trustees will recognize this. The irony is that the closure of NYUonline and Fathom was so easy because the companies were so disconnected from faculty or, stated otherwise, so squarely within the faculty's zone of indifference. Tighter coupling, ironically, will make closure more difficult.

FUTURE RESEARCH

The Role of the President

The role of the president in the creation and management of for-profit subsidiaries was curious. Though each company represented a significant political and financial investment by the university, none of the presidents was deeply involved in the subsidiary's operations; instead, whether as a matter of style or strategy, each president played no role or remained largely on the periphery. With Fathom and NYUonline, this detachment may have had significant implications for the subsidiaries.

Direct involvement and overt support of the subsidiaries, particularly for NYUonline and Fathom, might have helped strengthen each company's claim that it was consistent with the parent's mission. Conversely, "because college constituents recognize the legitimacy of administrative authority," (Birnbaum, 1992, p. 153), each president's lack of direct and visible involvement in the affairs of the subsidiary, particularly when under attack (e.g., Fathom), may have bolstered critics' claims that the subsidiary was illegitimate and antithetical to the university's mission. The president's outward aloofness may have signaled to participants that the subsidiary was outside the scope of the institution's core mission and values. Would direct presidential advocacy have made a difference for Fathom and NYUonline? What is the appropriate role of the president vis-à-vis the for-profit subsidiary? Macomber remarked that the lack of visible support from NYU's president contributed to NYUonline's demise. What he longed for from NYU's president was "a few clear signals . . . in the morass of organizational messages" (Kanter, 1983, p. 298) that showed support for the subsidiary and gave it legitimacy with NYU's faculty. Viewing the president's role in innovation from a bird's eye perspective, one might consider, what role presidents play in innovation in higher education in general? How much do they stake personally in innovative and risky activities?

Likewise, the role of the parent university's board of trustees should be studied further. Should the subsidiary have a clear link to the board of trustees? If so, what is the most effective link between the two organizations via the trustees: trustees on the board, a link to trustee committees and direct reports by the subsidiary CEO to the board, or some other connection? The board's role in innovative activity in universities should also be examined. What impact does direct trustee involvement have on a university's innovative activities? How should trustees be optimally positioned to help innovation succeed? Are boards a conservative force or a stimulus for reform and innovation?

The Link between Congruity and Viability

This research, which questioned some broadly accepted prescriptions for fostering innovation, invites several lines of future inquiry. First, the study concluded that the economic viability of academic subsidiaries increased with cultural congruity with the parent. This concept runs counter to business literature and contradicts one of the central assumptions in the creation of these subsidiaries. To better understand the relationship between viability and congruity, this matter should be studied further. What connections between the subsidiary and its parent will increase viability, yet not handcuff the subsidiary in the marketplace? How can an academic subsidiary be tightly coupled to faculty yet retain the necessary independence to meet market demand? What are the crucial connections between parent and subsidiary in governance, operations, and management?

Second, this study demonstrated the value of subsidiary leadership that understood academic culture and were accepted and trusted by faculty. The commercialization of higher education institutions begs the larger question of whether individuals with business backgrounds can effectively lead colleges and universities. A business leader may intuitively seem right for a business-like academy, but because of academic culture, this may not be the case. What are the variables that determine the type of leader who will be most effective for a particular institution or situation? How is the career profile of college and university presidents changing as the institutions they lead strive to be more effective in the marketplace?

Finally, faculty played a key role in these subsidiaries. The connection to faculty, or lack thereof, was a critical determinant of each company's trajectory. Faculty provide a conservative cultural force that can impede change in response to external demands. As they protect traditional academic values, they limit innovation. This conundrum raises the question of whether innovation that runs counter to faculty norms and values can be nurtured and thrive in academic organizations. Where has there been wide scale innovation in the academy and what role did faculty play? In response to this problem, Gumport (2000) has called for both change and continuity; for higher education and particularly faculty, to simultaneously "protect" traditional values and "respond" to emerging demands (p. 88, see also Kezar & Eckel, 2002). Yet, how can faculty foster change and innovation and simultaneously maintain cherished beliefs and values? How can faculty be a force for continuity, but also advance (or at least not retard) needed adjustment? These questions are central to the success of for-profit subsidiaries in higher education and in any significant change affecting the academic core of universities.

Research in each of these areas would add to our understanding of innovation, particularly at the intersection of the nonprofit and for-profit sectors and also provide important strategic and operational insights to academic leaders.

Appendix A

This appendix describes the research design and methodology and includes the following sections: 1) research questions and propositions, 2) research design, 3) data collection, 4) data analysis, 5) reliability, trustworthiness, and ethical considerations, 6) limitations of the research.

RESEARCH QUESTIONS AND PROPOSITIONS

Because the public debate and popular literature about for-profit subsidiaries chiefly concerns values and beliefs, I used organizational culture as the theoretical lens to consider the following research questions:

- *Why did the institution choose the form of a for-profit subsidiary to offer certain educational programs?*
- *What are the governance structures and processes of the for-profit subsidiary and why were they designed that way?*
  - *How does governance of the for-profit subsidiary occur in practice?*
- *How do the governance structures and processes of the for-profit subsidiary reflect or diverge from the culture and values of its non-profit parent institution?*
  - *How does this degree of congruence or divergence affect the decisions and actions of the for-profit subsidiary?*

Case study design "requires theoretical propositions. . . . Theory development prior to the collection of any case study data is an essential step. . . ." (Yin, 1994), p. 28). Based on the literature and also on a pilot study I conducted (Bleak, 2001), I developed the following propositions (Miles & Huberman, 1994; Yin, 1994):

1. For-profit subsidiaries were primarily established to access capital markets, but also with the intent to circumvent traditional academic governance structures. This was done either to achieve efficiency in governance and/or

to avoid cultural incongruities between the parent institution and its subsidiary.

2. Regardless of intent, for-profit subsidiaries will be governance hybrids, incorporating elements of the academy and corporation. The degree of hybridization, however, will be mediated by the level of congruence between the culture of the parent institution and its subsidiary.

3. The greater the congruity of culture between the for-profit subsidiary and its parent institution, the more the governance of the subsidiary will be within the parent institution's conventional structure of power and control. The less congruity, the more control will reside outside conventional governance and, specifically, outside faculty control.

Because I attempted "to make sense of [a] situation without imposing pre-existing expectations on the phenomenon" (Patton, 1990, p. 44), these propositions, or "hunches" (Mallon, 2000, p. 57) were intended not to predict the outcome of my research, but only to provide a "theoretical structure" (Hartley, 1994, p. 217), while still leaving flexibility during analysis.

RESEARCH DESIGN

The purpose of this research was to identify, describe, and compare the governance processes and structures of four for-profit subsidiaries of nonprofit universities. Qualitative research methods were appropriate because governance is a complex and dynamic process, not a static outcome (Merriam, 1988). Qualitative methods are particularly useful for descriptive analysis of organizations and allow "first-hand inspection of on-going organizational life" (Maanen, Dabbs, & Faulkner, 1982, p. 15–16). In addition, qualitative processes permit exploratory research of organizational phenomena, like governance, which are difficult to quantify (Marshall & Rossman, 1989; Merriam, 1988; Patton, 1990).

I used case study methodology which permits in-depth analysis (Merriam, 1988; Patton, 1990) and the study of complex processes that are difficult, if not impossible, to quantify or control (Baldridge, 1971b).

> Case studies are particularly valuable when the evaluation aims to capture individual differences or unique variations from one program setting to another, or from one program experience to another . . . [A] qualitative case study seeks to describe that unit in depth and detail, in context, and holistically. (Patton, 1990, p. 54)

The case study is a classic method for in depth study. This approach was suitable because my research was exploratory, and the analysis of dynamic processes was at the heart of my investigation (Baldridge, 1971b). For governance, especially viewed through the lens of organizational culture, case studies are particularly relevant, and enable "thick description" (Chaffee & Tierney, 1988, p. 13) and a "multifaceted interpretation" (p. 5).

Multiple case studies also allow comparisons and contrasts among organizations and events (Merriam, 1988).

> One aim of studying multiple cases is to increase generalizability, reassuring yourself that the events and processes in one well-described setting are not wholly idiosyncratic. At a deeper level, the aim is to see processes and outcomes across many cases, to understand how they are qualified by local conditions, and thus to develop more sophisticated descriptions and more powerful explanations. (Miles & Huberman, 1994, p. 172)

Conducting four case studies allowed me to identify themes and patterns across institutions and processes, while building explanations, and provided a richer view of the relationships between the parents and subsidiary organizations and their governance processes (Yin, 1994). Multiple cases permitted a deeper exploration of the subsidiary's organizational and environmental contexts and allowed me to examine both typicality and extremity (Hartley, 1994; Patton, 1990), with "the parallels and differences between them often [provoking] useful insights" (Baldridge, 1971b, p. 32).

Unit of Analysis

The unit of analysis in a case study can be an event, process, program, organization, or concept (Miles & Huberman, 1994). For this study, the unit of analysis was the governance processes and structures at four for-profit subsidiaries of non-profit universities. (See Appendix B for the specific governance structures and processes analyzed.) Rosenblatt, Rogers, and Nord (1993, p. 86) noted, "The critical issue for a governance framework is who participates in decisions and how they interact." In addition, Hult and Walcott (1990) commented that governance consisted of matters related to mission, primary organizational activities, and decision-making. In investigating governance, I considered the subsidiary board's composition, bylaws, and decision-making process. I determined the extent and nature of faculty participation in the subsidiary's governance by considering the role (or absence) of faculty governing boards, and what role faculty had in decision-making about programs, course content, and academic personnel. I determined who set the subsidiary's mission and the metrics used to measure its performance. In addition, I analyzed reporting relationships and channels of communication within the subsidiary and between the for-profit subsidiary and parent institution, and considered what decisions made in the subsidiary were subject to review by the parent.

When examining governance processes, I probed to understand whether and, if so, to what degree, divergence from the dominant norms of the parent institution influenced or shaped actual decisions, actions, and responses in the subsidiary. I did this by collecting data on critical decision/action incidents and by asking what considerations, from practical to political to moral, most affected the thinking of the decision makers. (See Appendix C for interview protocol.)

Sample

In choosing the four institutions, I used a criteria-sampling strategy (Miles & Huberman, 1994), applying the following criteria: (1) the for-profit subsidiary was established by a non-profit college or university; (2) the for-profit subsidiary had an established organizational structure and was in operation for at least six months; (3) the president of the university and the CEO of the subsidiary and most key leaders of both organizations were accessible to interview and have granted their permission. In addition, I restricted my study to private colleges and universities because of significant and intrinsic differences in the governance of public and private institutions.

In late 2000, when I began my study, there were approximately nine institutions that fit the first three criteria. (See Appendix D for complete list of for-profit subsidiaries.) However, four of these were public institutions. I sent a written request for access to the president of each of the other five institutions. I also contacted the CEO of each subsidiary with a similar letter. A week later in follow-up phone conversations, I received permission to study Babson College, Columbia University, Duke University, and New York University, and their for-profit subsidiaries. (See Appendix E for institutional comparisons.) The president of the fifth university demurred.

Selecting Informants

For each site, I compiled a list of potential interviewees. (See Table A-1.) I aimed to interview key participants in the governance of both the parent and the subsidiary, including those who were involved in the decision to create the for-profit subsidiary, those who were centrally involved in the company's operation and governance, and where available, the most influential critics of the new organization. With the help of the president of the university or his designate, I contacted each individual by email to request an interview.

Table A-1. List of Potential Interviewees by Position

For-profit subsidiary	University or college
Chair / members of the board of directors	Chair / members of the board of trustees
Chief executive officer	President
Chief financial officer	Provost or chief academic officer
Chief operations officer	Other major liaisons or supervisors of the subsidiary (including relevant deans)
Other key managers	Key faculty involved with subsidiary
Leader of faculty governance body, if one exists	Chair of the faculty senate or the nominal leader of the shared governance body on the faculty side
Other key informants identified through snowballing technique	Other key informants identified through snowballing technique

To broaden my informant list, I asked each interviewee to name other informants (e.g., administrators, faculty members, or board members). This method for finding "information-rich key informants" (Patton, 1990, p. 176) is called a snowballing or chain technique (Bogdan & Biklen, 1992; Seidman, 1998), and ensures "that the research methodology slices vertically through the organization, obtaining data from multiple levels and perspectives" (Leonard-Barton, 1995, p. 40). Through this technique I was able to identify at least two additional informants at each research site.

To eliminate key informant biases (Maxwell, 1996), I reviewed institutional documents to identify other informants, particularly those who were critical of the subsidiary's governance and its existence. Through this method, I identified additional informants.

DATA COLLECTION

I collected data from three sources: in-depth interviews, institutional documents, and external documents related to the governance of these four for-profit subsidiaries.

Interviews

Data were collected through in-depth, semi-structured interviews (Yin, 1994). I followed the same interview protocol for each institution, with distinct lines of inquiry for faculty and for administrators of the university and subsidiary. (See Appendix C for interview protocol.)

At the outset of each interview, I described the purpose of my research and of the interview and then asked a series of general questions to elicit the story of how and why the for-profit subsidiary was created. Next, I asked questions concerning the governance of each subsidiary and its parent. The answers to these questions illuminated both the structure and process of governance in practice. The interview concluded with questions designed to uncover aspects of each organization's culture and values. The semi-structured interview design allowed me to probe additional issues informants raised, and the open-ended questions enabled me to gather the informant's point of view without predetermining important elements of governance or culture (Patton, 1990).

I interviewed 42 people in all: eight at Babson College / Babson Interactive, eleven at Columbia University / Fathom, thirteen at Duke University / Duke Corporate Education, and ten at NYU / NYUonline. Supplemental data were collected through seven follow-up interviews (four in person and three by phone) to clarify events and to provide corroboration (Marshall & Rossman, 1989). I interviewed the president of the university at two sites, the provost or academic vice president at each site, the CEO of each subsidiary, members of both institution's governing boards, managers of the subsidiary and chief administrative officers of the parent, and faculty senate leaders and key faculty members. (See Appendix F for complete list of informants interviewed.)

I continued interviewing until I reached a point of sufficiency in data collection and saturation of information (Seidman, 1998), when I was not "gaining significantly new knowledge or ideas about the focus of [my] study" (Hartley, 1994, p. 219).

Almost all of the interviews were conducted at the workplace of the informant and lasted approximately 60 minutes; however, I conducted six interviews by phone because of scheduling difficulties. All but two of the interviews were audio-taped, all with the approval of the informant, and later transcribed verbatim. The two interviews that were not audio-taped were conducted over the phone. For these interviews I relied on hand-written notes; for all other interviews, hand-written notes supplemented the audio recording.

Written Documentation

I collected both internal and external written documentation from informants and from public sources. These documents supplemented the collection of interview data and were also used to triangulate the data, and thus increase the validity of my research (Patton, 1990). These documents allowed me to confirm existing themes and search for new themes as well as clarify the order of events. Examples of this documentation follow.

Institutional documents:

- Articles of incorporation for subsidiaries
- Operating agreement between subsidiary and parent organization
- Board of Trustees and other advisory board bylaws and minutes
- Strategic planning documents
- Documents describing budgetary process and procedures
- Budgets
- Governance policy manuals and handbooks
- Administrative memoranda/letters
- Minutes from faculty senate meetings and other faculty committees
- Personnel recruitment literature

External documents:

- Newspaper articles
- Letters to the editor in student/campus newspapers, local and national newspapers, and *The Chronicle of Higher Education*
- Reports and research provided by investment and financial research companies
- Articles and reports from sources on the Internet tracking the for-profit higher education industry
- Each informant was also asked to identify additional sources of written documentation.

DATA ANALYSIS

"Data analysis is . . . a messy, ambiguous, time-consuming, and fascinating process." At its essence, it is "a process of bringing order, structure, and meaning to the mass of collected data" (Marshall & Rossman, 1989, p. 112). I proceeded as follows:

Data management and organization

Data were managed in a systematic way. All audio-recorded interviews were transcribed following the interviews, both electronic and hard copies of each interview were maintained, and all written documentation was filed. In addition, I also used a qualitative analysis software package, Atlas.ti, to manage all electronic data.

Generating Categories, Themes, and Patterns

To make sense of the immense amount of data that was collected, I employed several strategies suggested by qualitative methodologists: (1) Developing coding strategies (Maxwell, 1996; Miles & Huberman, 1994); (2) writing regular memos to myself (Maxwell, 1996); (3) developing a stand-alone case study for each organization (Patton, 1990); and (4) using a multi-case comparison and cross-case analysis (Maxwell, 1996; Seidman, 1998).

In order to make sense of the data, I used a coding strategy to identify "recurring regularities," themes, and patterns (Guba, 1978). I read and coded each interview transcript (sometimes rereading and coding several times), collapsing and combining codes, as appropriate, and as broader themes and categories emerged from the data. This iterative process allowed me to continuously develop and test emerging hypotheses (Marshall & Rossman, 1989). I used the qualitative analysis software to code each interview and to organize and retrieve codes.

In order to test emerging hypotheses and propositions against the data, I wrote regular analytic memos to myself. These memos captured my own thinking and insights and compared the meaning I was attributing to the data with the actual data (Maxwell, 1996; Miles & Huberman, 1994).

I developed a stand-alone case study for each for-profit subsidiary to better understand each institution in context (Maxwell, 1996). These case studies helped me to realize more fully what I knew and also still needed to learn about each institution, and helped me understand the "idiosyncratic manifestation" of governance and culture at each institution and subsidiary (Patton, 1990, p. 387). Only parts of these stand-alone cases are presented in this book; however, more complete cases on NYUonline and Babson Interactive can be found in a qualifying paper I produced to fulfill my doctoral degree requirements (Bleak, 2001) and in a teaching case I wrote on Duke Corporate Education for the Harvard Institutes for Higher Education (Bleak, 2001, June).

From the individual case studies and coding schemata, I developed a multi-case comparison to analyze similarities and differences across the four sites. The themes generated from this comparison comprise chapters 2 through 5.

RELIABILITY, TRUSTWORTHINESS, AND ETHICAL CONSIDERATIONS

To increase the trustworthiness of my study, I triangulated data by method and source by collecting data through a variety of sources—including interviews and internal and external documents—and by interviewing people at varied levels of each organization (Patton, 1990). Throughout data analysis, pursuant to Maxwell (1996) and Patton (1990), I remained aware of and looked for discrepant evidence and rival explanations that would contradict my analysis and challenge emerging conclusions. I also sought the feedback of knowledgeable peers and colleagues throughout my study. I shared my findings regularly with my ad hoc committee of readers, particularly my chair, and with a peer dissertation study group. I also presented my analysis and preliminary findings at two academic conferences, where I received feedback and thoughtful questions.

Based on these safeguards, I have confidence in producing extrapolations (Patton, 1990) from this study. Extrapolations are not generalizations, but "modest speculations on the likely applicability of findings to other situations under similar, but not identical, conditions. Extrapolations are logical, thoughtful, and problem oriented rather than statistical and probabilistic" (Patton, 1990, p. 489).

LIMITATIONS OF THE RESEARCH

I chose to use case study design because it was the best and most appropriate method for answering my research questions. However, this method also has drawbacks. Because case studies produce a plethora of data, in analyzing this data and generating conclusions, researchers may oversimplify or exaggerate a situation (Guba & Lincoln, 1981). In addition, because "the researcher is the primary instrument of data collection and analysis" (Merriam, 1988, p. 34), the study is subject to the researcher's personal biases. Though this is a valid concern, all investigative methods are subject to researcher bias and error. Through my research design and methods for assuring reliability and validity, I sought to minimize the impact of my own biases and to remain sensitive to oversimplifications and exaggerations.

The influence of the researcher in a study can never be fully eliminated (Maxwell, 1996), and I acknowledge that the interviews I conducted could have affected the informants (Patton, 1990). To minimize this influence however, I tried to interact with the people I spoke with in a natural and trustful manner (Bogdan & Biklen, 1992).

Finally, just keeping pace with events in these companies was difficult. Throughout the course of this research, all four companies were reorganizing in an effort to meet the demands of the market and achieve profitability. In addition, personnel in the parent institutions were in flux. What and who was seen at one point would often change later. This presented difficulties in interpreting the meaning and significance of events and demanded that the time frame of this study be carefully bounded. Despite these difficulties, the fluid situation had positive effects on the research. First, each company's efforts to respond internally to organizational needs and externally to the demands of its environment highlighted the processes of governance and cultural development. Second, during the course of the study, two subsidiaries, NYUonline and Fathom, ceased operations and closed. NYUonline's closing in January 2002 allowed me to observe the company's complete life cycle. I conducted interviews with key participants regarding the company's demise. Unfortunately, I was not able to do this with Fathom because it closed while writing this material, after my research and analysis was complete. Because of the traumatic nature of NYUonline's closure on employees and others involved with the company, I was cognizant of the disadvantages of "retrospective event histories" noted by Glick, et al. (1995):

Responses may be associated with errors of recall; for example, informants may selectively neglect some events that are important or focus on trends that are actually unimportant but are temporarily conspicuous to the informant. . . . Errors of recall can result from strong cognitive processes such as rationalization, self-presentation, simplification, attribution, and simple lapses of memory. (p. 139)

I minimized these concerns to some degree by interviewing numerous people at the sight following the closing of the company, and by collecting and analyzing written documentation to corroborate informants' recall of events.

Appendix B

UNIT OF ANALYSIS: GOVERNANCE STRUCTURES AND PROCESSES

Governance structures are the formal and informal entities that have and use legitimate power, or authority, in the organization. Thus, structure is the architecture of governance. Governance processes encompass the decisions and actions (i.e., the dynamics) through which legitimate power is exercised in the organization.

Table B-1.

Structures	Processes
Board of Trustees or Board of Directors	Decision-making and review
Formal and ad hoc board committees	Resource allocation
Board bylaws	Performance evaluation
Faculty Senate	Appointments, promotion, and curriculum review
Formal and ad hoc faculty committees	Program approval
University administration (e.g., President, President's Cabinet, Dean's Council)	Communication and dissemination of information
Organizational hierarchy	Policy approval
Formal reporting lines and scope of authority	Strategic planning
	Mission determination

Appendix C

INTERVIEW PROTOCOL

General Questions to be asked of *all* interviewees
General overview questions:

- Who decided to create [for-profit subsidiary]?
- Why was [for-profit subsidiary] established? Why did you choose the governance structure you have for the subsidiary? Why was the for-profit structure chosen instead of the non-profit organizational form?
- What has this structure enabled you to do that would have been difficult or impossible if the subsidiary were treated like any other unit of the university?

Questions *only* for For-Profit subsidiary management and University administration (including governing boards)
Governance questions:

- Think of an important policy or strategic decision that was made recently in [for-profit subsidiary], how was this decision made? Who was involved and at what level in this decision and its implementation? What considerations affected the thinking of the decision makers?
- What principles are taken into account when making decisions in [for-profit subsidiary]? Are these the same principles that are considered in decision making in [university]?
- In your opinion, who are the really influential people in [for-profit subsidiary/university]? (Harrison, 1994)
- What are the [university] board of trustees' responsibilities in the governance of [for-profit subsidiary]?

- What are the responsibilities of the [for-profit subsidiary's] board of directors?
- What are the president/CEO's responsibilities?
- What are the responsibilities of the faculty?
- What items come under review by the [university] board of trustees?
- Who decides the budget in [for-profit subsidiary]? Who controls budget surpluses and who is at risk in case of a budget shortfall? Who sets compensation levels for [for-profit subsidiary]?
- Can [for-profit subsidiary's] CEO take significant action in administrative and budgetary matters without consulting the board of directors? Is there a faculty governing board at [for-profit subsidiary]? If so, what are its responsibilities?
- Can [for-profit subsidiary's] CEO take significant action with regard to courses/curriculum without consulting the faculty governing board? To what degree does [for-profit subsidiary] have to take account of faculty opinions?
- Who does the subsidiary's CEO report to? What is the reporting relationship between the subsidiary's board of directors and the university's board of trustees?
- Have there been any major conflicts between [university] and [for-profit subsidiary]? If so, what was at issue and what was the outcome? Was there a clash of values?
- What has been the most difficult situation you have faced in governing [for-profit subsidiary]?

Values questions:

- If you were telling a friend what it was really like to work here, how would you describe the atmosphere? (Harrison, 1994)
- What aspects of work are most emphasized here? Are there difficulties and barriers to getting the work done here or to doing it the way you would like? (Harrison, 1994)
- What do you think are the core values of [for-profit subsidiary]? Do these core values differ for [university]? If so, in what ways?
- What is the mission of [for-profit subsidiary]? How is this different from [university's] mission?
- Who chose/decided the mission of [for-profit subsidiary]? How does the organization pursue its mission? (Harrison, 1994)

Questions *only* for Faculty

Governance questions:

- What three adjectives or short phrases best capture for you the character and quality of governance on this campus?
- What role(s) do faculty play in governance at [university]? What specific role do you play?
- Please describe briefly the faculty's actual role and what you would judge as its appropriate role in these specific areas of decision-making in [university]:
    - Setting the curriculum, that is, deciding what courses get taught and what majors are offered
    - Appointing new faculty
    - Evaluating current faculty
    - Setting individual faculty salaries (i.e., determining raises)
    - Promoting faculty
    - Setting institutional priorities
    - Setting operating budgets
    - Setting admissions criteria and standards
- In your opinion, is [university] committed to shared governance? How is this commitment exhibited?
- Who are the really influential people in [university]? (Harrison, 1994)
- What are the general responsibilities of faculty in [for-profit subsidiary]? What is your role in the company?
- Is there a faculty governing board at [for-profit subsidiary]? If so, what are its responsibilities?
- Can [for-profit subsidiary's] CEO take significant action with regard to courses/curriculum without consulting the faculty governing board? To what degree does [for-profit subsidiary] have to take account of faculty opinions?
- What principles are taken into account when making decisions in [for-profit subsidiary]? Are these the same principles that are considered in decision making in [university]?

Values questions:

- If you were telling a friend what it was really like to work at [university], how would you describe the atmosphere? (Harrison, 1994)

- What aspects of work are most emphasized here? Are there difficulties and barriers to getting the work done here or to doing it the way you would like? (Harrison, 1994)
- What do you think are the core values of [university]? Do these core values differ for [for-profit subsidiary]? If so, in what ways?
- What is the mission of [university]? How is this different from [for-profit subsidiary's] mission?
- Have there been any major conflicts between [university] and [for-profit subsidiary]? If so, what was at issue and what was the outcome? Was there a clash of values?

Questions to be answered through written documents before conducting interviews:

- Who is on the board of directors of [for-profit subsidiary]? Who is the chair?
- How were these directors chosen?
- Who appoints the chair of the board?
- Does the board set term limits for directors?
- Is there a seat on the board reserved for a faculty member?
- How often does the board of directors meet?
- Are director's compensated for their service?
- What are the board of directors' main activities (i.e., What is the board's emphasis?)?

Appendix D

Table D-1: Roster of current for-profit subsidiaries created by universities to deliver and market online distance education

For-Profit Subsidiary	Parent Institution	Purpose	URL	Founding of For-Profit	Institutional Control
NYUOnline Inc.	New York University	Provides career focused courses, certificate programs, and knowledge management consulting to companie and individuals	nyuonline.com	1998 (closed January 2002)	Private
UMUConline.com	University of Maryland University College	Established to market online courses	umuconline.com	1999 (for profit structure abandoned Oct. 2001)	Public
Class.com	University of Nebraska	Provides online courses to high school students	class.com	1999	Public
Virtual Temple	Temple University	Established to market Temple's online course offerings	(no website)	1999 (closed July 2001)	Public
Indiana Partners	University of Indiana, Kelley School of Management	Provides tailored educational services to corporations, including consulting and courses	(undetermined)	1999	Public
Fathom	Columbia University	"interactive knowledge site"	fathom.com	2000 (closed January 2003)	Private

Table D-1: Roster of current for-profit subsidiaries created by universities to deliver and market online distance education (continued)

For-Profit Subsidiary	Parent Institution	Purpose	URL	Founding of For-Profit	Institutional Control
ECornell	Cornell University	Established to market and deliver online courses	ecornell.com	2000	Private
Duke Corporate Education Inc.	Duke University, Fuqua School of Business	Provides tailored educational services to corporations, including consulting and courses	dukece.com	2000	Private
Babson Interactive Inc.	Babson College	Provides non-degree and degree granting business courses to corporations—the online component of executive education	(no website)	2000	Private
Global Film School Inc.	UCLA	Provides online film classes	globalfilmschool.com	Jan. 2001	Public

This list represents, as of January 21, 2002, the for-profit subsidiaries that have been created to deliver and market online distance education.

Appendix E

Table E-1: Comparison of the four research sites

Institution	Location	Carnegie Classification	Total Enrollment (Fall 2002)	For-Profit Subsidiary	Founding of Subsidiary	Institutional Control
New York University	Manhattan, New York City	Doctoral/Research Universities—Extensive	51,901[1]	NYUOnline Inc.	1998 (closed January 2002)	Private
Columbia University	Manhattan,	Doctoral/Research Universities—Extensive	20,028[2]	Fathom, Inc.	2000 (closed	Private
Duke University	Durham, North Carolina	Doctoral/Research Universities—Extensive	11,504[3]	Duke Corporate Education Inc.	2000	Private
Babson College	Wellesley, Massachusetts	Schools of Business and Management	3,431[4]	Babson Interactive, LLC	2000	Private

[1]Headcount enrollment, (14,751 of the 51,951 students enrolled are in non-credit programs); http://www.nyu.edu/search.nyu
[2]FTE enrollment; http://www.columbia.edu/cu/opir/2003EnrlPTFT.htm
[3]FTE enrollment; http://www.finsvc.duke.edu/finsvc/Resources/reports/financial_reports02.pdf
[4]FTE enrollment; http://www2.babson.edu/babson/BabsonHPp.nsf/Public/aboutBabsonglance#Student

Appendix F

INFORMANTS INTERVIEWED

Columbia University / Fathom (11 informants)

George Rupp	Columbia University President
Jonathan Cole	Columbia University Provost; Fathom Academic Council chair
Michael Crow	Columbia University Executive Vice Provost; Fathom board of directors
Elizabeth Irvin	Columbia University General Counsel
Richard Bulliet	Columbia professor; co-chair of University Senate subcommittee (phone interview)
Sharyn O'Halloran	Columbia professor; co- chair of University Senate subcommittee (phone interview)
Kate Wittenberg	Columbia University director of Electronic Publishing Initiative; member of University Senate subcommittee (phone interview)
Ann Kirschner	Fathom CEO; Fathom board of directors
Anne Rollow	Fathom Vice President for Business Development
David Wolff	Fathom Vice President
Ryan Craig	Fathom Vice President

Babson College / Babson Interactive (8 informants)

Michael Fetters	Babson College vice president for academics (2 interviews)
Ron Weiner	Babson College trustee; Babson Interactive board of directors (phone interview)
P. J. Guinan	Babson College professor; Babson Interactive board of directors
Allen Cohen	Babson College professor

Bill Lawler	Babson College professor
Fred Nanni	Babson College professor
Thomas Moore	Babson Interactive CEO; Babson Interactive board of directors; Babson College Dean of Executive Education (2 interviews)
Stephen Laster	Babson Interactive Chief Information Officer

NYU / NYUonline (10 informants)

Harvey Stedman	NYU Provost; NYUonline board of directors
David Finney	NYU Dean of SCPS; NYUonline board of directors (2 interviews)
Robert Manuel	NYU employee; former NYUonline manager
Stuart Hirsch	NYU professor (phone)
Carl Lebowitz	NYU professor and chair of University Senate (phone interview)
Gordon Macomber	NYUonline CEO (2 interviews)
Lloyd Short	NYUonline executive (2 interviews)
Dan Daniel	NYUonline executive
David Hawthorne	NYUonline executive
Jeff Tagliabue	NYUonline executive

Duke University / Duke Corporate Education (13 informants)

Nan Keohane	Duke University President
Peter Lange	Duke University Provost; Duke CE board of directors
Tallman Trask	Duke University Executive Vice President; Duke CE board of directors
John Payne	Fuqua Associate Dean
Allan Lind	Fuqua professor
Blair Sheppard	Duke CE President and CEO; Duke CE board of directors (3 interviews)
Judy Rosenblum	Duke CE Executive Vice President (phone interview)
Wanda Wallace	Duke CE Executive Vice President
John Gallagher	Duke CE Vice President; former Fuqua professor
John McCann	Duke CE executive; Fuqua professor
Bob Reinheimer	Duke CE academic council; former Fuqua professor (phone interview)
Sim Sitkin	Duke CE academic council; Fuqua professor
Barbara Frick	Duke CE controller; secretary to the board of directors

Notes

NOTES TO CHAPTER ONE

1. Ironically, later *The New England Journal of Medicine* loosened its policy, citing the difficulty of finding authors with appropriate connections to write review articles and editorials. The new policy adds "significant" to the statement regarding an author's financial interest in a company (Guterman, 2002, June 13).
2. Ultimately the dispute was settled in the University of California at San Francisco's favor, with Immune Response Corporation agreeing to give research data they had withheld (Guterman & Werf, 2001, October 5). The company was later named in a class-action lawsuit accusing it of inflating its stock price by misrepresenting the drug's prospects (Van Der Werf, 2001, September 13).

NOTES TO CHAPTER TWO

1. The New York University School of Continuing and Professional Studies, with an annual enrollment of approximately 60,000 students, is the largest institution of its kind in the nation. Close to 80 percent of enrolled students work full-time; most are between the ages of 25 and 45. The School offers more than 2,000 credit and non-credit courses, many of these online through its "Virtual College."
2. Gerald Heeger left NYU to become the president of the University of Maryland—University College. Upon assuming the presidency, he created UMUConline.com, a for-profit subsidiary created to market and deliver online education.
3. Christensen (1997, p. xv) defines disruptive technology as "innovations that result in worse product performance, at least in the near-term." Many consider the Internet to be a disruptive technology for higher education because it brings "to a market a very different value proposition than had been available previously," eventually creating competitive difficulties for institutions that were successful using traditional ways of creating products (or of delivering education as in the current case), which Christensen calls "sustaining technologies" (p. xv). Chapter 4 contains a further discussion

of Christensen's work on disruptive technologies as it applies to for-profit subsidiaries in higher education.

NOTES TO CHAPTER THREE

1. Higdon resigned as President of Babson College, June 30, 2001. His successor, Brian Barefoot, chose not to be a member of Babson Interactive's board in order to avoid any conflict of interest.
2. Board membership as of July 1, 2002. http://www.duke.edu/web/ous/trusteesgood.htm

Bibliography

AAUP. (1990). Statement on Government of Colleges and Universities. Retrieved October 30, 2000, from http://www.aaup.org/govern.htm

Abbott, W. F. (1974, March). Prestige and Goals in American Universities. *Social Forces, 52*(3), 401–407.

Abel, D. (2000a, October 19). Answers Pending for UMass Plan to go Online. *Boston Globe,* p. B1.

Abel, D. (2000b, June 15). UMass weighs Internet Push. *The Boston Globe,* pp. A1, A21.

Abeles, T. P. (2002, August 2). Letter to the Editor. *The Chronicle of Higher Education,* p. B14.

AGB. (1996). *Renewing the Academic Presidency: Stronger Leadership for Tougher Times.* Washington, D.C.: Association of Governing Boards of Universities and Colleges.

AGB. (1998). *AGB Statement on Institutional Governance.* Washington, D.C.: Association of Governing Boards of Universities and Colleges.

Ahuja, A. (2001, May 7). When Corporate Cash Corrupts. *The Times.*

Allen, D. N., & Norling, F. (1991). Exploring Perceived Threats in Faculty Commercialization of Research. In A. M. Brett, D. V. Gibson & R. W. Smilor (Eds.), *University Spin-off Companies: Economic Development, Faculty Entrepreneurs, and Technology Transfer* (pp. 85–102). New York: Rowman & Litchfield Publishers, Inc.

Altschuler, G. C. (2001, August 5). The E-Learning Curve. *The New York Times,* p. 13.

Apollo. (2002). *Apollo Group, Inc. 2002 Annual Report.* Phoenix, AZ.

Arenson, K. W. (2000, August 2). Columbia Leads Academic Pack in Turning Profit From Research. *The New York Times,* pp. A1, A25.

Arnold, D. R., & Capella, L. M. (1985). Corporate Culture and the Marketing Concept: A Diagnostic Instrument for Utilities. *Public Utilities Fortnightly, 118*(8), 32–38.

Arnone, M. (2002a, May 10). Columbia Senate Questions Spending on Fathom. *The Chronicle of Higher Education,* p. A41.

Arnone, M. (2002b, February 22). Fathom Adds Training to Distance-Education Offerings. *The Chronicle of Higher Education,* p. A27.

Arnone, M. (2002c, April 25). Report from Columbia University's Senate Sharply Criticizes Spending for Online Venture. *The Chronicle of Higher Education.*

Austin, A. E. (1990). Faculty Cultures, Faculty Values. In W. Tierney, G. (Ed.), *Assessing Academic Climates and Cultures* (pp. 61–74). San Francisco: Jossey-Bass Publishers.

Babson. (2001). A History of Babson College in Timeline. Retrieved April 13, 2001, from http://www.babson.edu/archives/timeline.htm

Bailey, T., Badway, N., & Gumport, P. J. (2001). *For-Profit Higher Education and Community Colleges.* Stanford, CA: National Center for Postsecondary Improvement.

Baldridge, J. V. (1971a). *Academic Governance.* Berkeley, CA: McCutchan Publishing.

Baldridge, J. V. (1971b). *Power and Conflict in the University: Research in the Sociology of Complex Organizations.* New York: John Wiley and Sons.

Baldridge, J. V., Curtis, D. V., Ecker, G., & Riley, G. L. (1978). *Policy Making and Effective Leadership: A National Study of Academic Management.* San Francisco: Jossey-Bass Publishers.

Baldridge, J. V., Curtis, D. V., Ecker, G. P., & Riley, G. L. (1977). Alternative Models of Governance in Higher Education. In G. Riley & J. V. Baldridge (Eds.), *Governing Academic Organizations.* Berkeley, CA: McCutchan Publishing.

Baldwin, R. G., & Leslie, D. W. (2001, Spring). Rethinking the Structure of Shared Governance. *AAC&U Peer Review, 3,* 18–19.

Becher, T. (1984). The Cultural View. In B. Clark (Ed.), *Perspectives in Higher Education.* Berkeley: University of California Press.

Benjamin, R., Carroll, S., Jacobi, M., Krop, C., & Shires, M. (1993). *The Redesign of Governance in Higher Education.* Santa Monica, CA: RAND.

Bensimon, E. M., & Neumann, A. (1993). *Redesigning Collegiate Leadership: Teams and Teamwork in Higher Education.* Baltimore: Johns Hopkins University Press.

Besse, R. M. (1973). A Comparison of the University with the Corporation. In J. A. Perkins (Ed.), *The University as an Organization* (pp. 107–120). New York: McGraw Hill Book Company.

Bird, B. J., & Allen, D. N. (1989). Faculty Entrepreneurship in Research University Environments. *Journal of Higher Education, 60*(5), 583–596.

Birnbaum, R. (1988). *How Colleges Work: The Cybernetics of Academic Organization and Leadership* (1st ed.). San Francisco: Jossey-Bass.

Birnbaum, R. (1992). *How Academic Leadership Works: Understanding Success and Failure in the College Presidency* (1st ed.). San Francisco: Jossey-Bass.

Birnbaum, R. (2000). *Management Fads in Higher Education: Where They Come From, What They Do, Why They Fail.* San Francisco: Jossey-Bass.

Blair, M. M. (1995). *Ownership and Control: Rethinking Corporate Governance for the Twenty-first Century.* Washington, D.C.: The Brookings Institution.

Bleak, J. L. (2001). *Structures and Values: The Governance of For-Profit Subsidiaries of Non-Profit Universities.* Unpublished Qualifying Paper, Harvard University Graduate School of Education, Cambridge, MA.

Bleak, J. L. (2001, June). *Duke Corporate Education, Inc.* Cambridge, MA: Harvard Institutes for Higher Education.

Blum, A. (2002, June 16). Online Ed Taking Off. *Boston Globe,* p. H1.

Blumenstyk, G. (2000, November 24). Universities Collected $641-million in Royalties on Inventions in 1999. *The Chronicle of Higher Education,* p. A49.

Blumenstyk, G. (2001, February 9). Knowledge Is 'a Form of Venture Capital' for a Top Columbia Administrator. *The Chronicle of Higher Education,* p. A29.

Blumenstyk, G. (2001, June 22). A Vilified Corporate Partnership Produces Little Change (Except Better Facilities). *The Chronicle of Higher Education,* pp. A24–27.

Blumenstyk, G. (2002, March 22). Income From University Licenses on Patents Exceeded $1—Billion. *The Chronicle of Higher Education,* p. A31.

Blumenthal, D., Gluck, M., Louis, K. S., & Wise, D. (1986). University-Industry Research Relationships in Biotechnology: Implications for the University. *Science, 232,* 1361–1366.

Bogdan, R. C., & Biklen, S. K. (1992). *Qualitative Research for Education.* Boston: Allyn & Bacon.

Bok, D. (2002). Preserving Educational Values. *Continuing Higher Education Review, 66,* 7–29.

Bowen, H. R., & Schuster, J. H. (1986). *American Professors: A National Resource Imperiled.* New York: Oxford University Press.

Bowen, W. G. (1994). *Inside the Boardroom: Governance by Directors and Trustees.* New York: John Wiley & Sons, Inc.

Bower, J. L. (1970). *Managing the Resource Allocation Process.* Boston: Harvard Business School Press.

Breneman, D. W. (1970). *The Doctor of Philosophy Production Process: A Study of Departmental Behavior.* Unpublished Dissertation, University of California— Berkeley, Berkeley, CA.

Breneman, D. W. (2002, June 14). For Colleges, This is Not Just Another Recession. *The Chronicle of Higher Education,* p. B7.

Brett, A. M., Gibson, D. V., & Smilor, R. W. (Eds.). (1991). *University Spin-off Companies: Economic Development, Faculty Entrepreneurs, and Technology Transfer.* New York: Rowman & LIttlefield Publishers, Inc.

Briefing. (2001). Education Stock Analysis. Retrieved November 8, 2001, from http://www.briefing.com

Carlin, J. (1999, November 5). Restoring Sanity to an Academic World Gone Mad. *The Chronicle of Higher Education,* p. A76.

Carlson, S. (2000a, April 14). A 1,000-acre Incubator for Research and Business. *The Chronicle of Higher Education,* pp. A49-A50, A52.

Carlson, S. (2000b, May 5). Going for Profit and Scholarship on the Web. *The Chronicle of Higher Education,* p. A45.

Carlson, S. (2001a, November 16). Columbia University's Fathom Seeks Users Among 'New Yorker' Readers. *The Chronicle of Higher Education,* p. A40.

Carlson, S. (2001b, February 9). For-Profit Web Venture Shifts Gears, Hoping to Find a Way to Make a Profit. *The Chronicle of Higher Education,* p. A33.

Carlson, S., & Carnevale, D. (2001, December 14). Debating the Demise of NYUonline. *The Chronicle of Higher Education,* p. A31.

Carnevale, D. (1999, October 22). Distance Education Can Bolster the Bottom Line, A Professor Argues. *The Chronicle of Higher Education,* p. A60.

Carnevale, D., & Young, J. R. (1999, December 17). Who Owns On-Line Courses? Colleges and Professors Start to Sort it Out. *The Chronicle of Higher Education,* p. A45.

Carr, S. (1999, December 17). For-profit Venture to Market Distance-education Courses Stirs Concern at Temple. *The Chronicle of Higher Education,* p. A46.

Carr, S. (2000a, March 4). Cornell Creates a For-profit Subsidiary to Market Distance-education Programs. *The Chronicle of Higher Education,* p. A47.

Carr, S. (2000b, December 15). A Day in the Life of a New Type of Professor. *The Chronicle of Higher Education,* p. A47.

Carr, S. (2000c, June 9). Faculty Members are Wary of Distance-education Ventures. *The Chronicle of Higher Education,* p. A41.

Carr, S., & Kiernan, V. (2000, April 14). For-Profit Web Venture Seeks to Replicate the University Experience Online. *The Chronicle of Higher Education,* p. A59.

Casselman, B. (2001, January 29). Committee Reports on Fathom's Difficulties. *Columbia Spectator.*

Chaffee, E. E., & Tierney, W. G. (1988). *Collegiate Culture and Leadership Strategies.* New York: Macmillan Publishing Co.

Chait, R. P. (2000). From unpublished address given at MIT. Cambridge, MA.

Chait, R. P. (2002). Does Faculty Governance Differ at Colleges with Tenure and Colleges without Tenure? In R. P. Chait (Ed.), *The Questions of Tenure* (pp. 69–100).

Chait, R. P., Holland, T. P., & Taylor, B. E. (1993). *The Effective Board of Trustees.* Phoenix, AZ: American Council on Education and The Oryx Press.

Christensen, C. M. (1997). *The Innovator's Dilemma: When New Technologies Cause Great Firms to Fail.* Boston: Harvard Business School Press.

Christensen, C. M., & Overdorf, M. (2000, March-April). Meeting the Challenge of Disruptive Change. *Harvard Business Review,* 67–76.

Christensen, C. M., & Shu, K. (1999). *What is an Organization's Culture?* Boston: Harvard Business School class discussion note.

Chronicle. (2000, July 14). Duke University's Business School is Forming a Private Venture to Provide Educational Services Tailored to Companies. *The Chronicle of Higher Education,* p. A34.

Clark, B. R. (1963). Faculty Organization and Authority. In T. F. Lunsford (Ed.), *The Study of Academic Administration* (pp. 37–51). Denver, CO: Western Interstate Commission for Higher Education.

Clark, B. R. (1972). The Organizational Saga in Higher Education. *Administrative Science Quarterly, 17,* 179–194.

Clark, B. R. (1980). *Academic Culture.*Unpublished manuscript, Yale University, Higher Education Research Group.

Clark, B. R. (1984). *The Higher Education System: Academic Organization in Cross-national Perspective.* Berkeley: University of California Press.

Clark, B. R. (1993). Faculty: Differentiation and Dispersion. In A. Levine (Ed.), *Higher Learning In America: 1980—2000* (pp. 163–178). Baltimore: The Johns Hopkins University Press.

CNN. (2002, August 29a). Apollo Group Inc. Reports Business Outlook for Fiscal 2003. Retrieved August 29, 2002, from http://money.cnn.com/services/ticker-headlines/bw/222410020.htm

CNN. (2002, August 29b). *Apollo Group, Inc.* Retrieved August 29, 2002, from http://money.cnn.com/MGI/snap/A0871.htm

Cohen, M. D., & March, J. G. (1974). *Leadership and Ambiguity: The American College President.* New York: McGraw-Hill Book Company.

Cohen, M. D., & March, J. G. (1986). *Leadership and Ambiguity: The American College President* (2nd ed.). Boston: Harvard Business School Press.

Cole, J. R. (1994). Balancing Acts: Dilemmas of Choice Facing Research Universities. In J. R. Cole, E. G. Barber & S. R. Graubard (Eds.), *The Research University in a Time of Discontent* (pp. 1–36). Baltimore: The Johns Hopkins University Press.

Cole, J. R. (2001, February 5). Fathom.com a Viable Technological Opportunity for Distance Learning. *Columbia Spectator.*

Collie, S. L., & Chronister, J. L. (2001, Spring). In Search of the Next Generation of Faculty Leaders. *AAC&U Peer Review, 3,* 22–23.

Collis, D. (2001). When Industries Change: The Future of Higher Education. *Continuing Higher Education Review, 65,* 7–24.

Columbia. (1999). A Brief History of Columbia. Retrieved December 19, 2002, from www.columbia.edu/cu/aboutcolumbia/history.html

Corcoran, M., & Clark, S. M. (1984). Professional Socialization and Contemporary Career Attitudes of Three Faculty Generations. *Research in Higher Education, 20,* 131–153.

Cox, A. M. (2000, October 30). Campus-Governance Meeting Raises Questions about the Applicability of the Business Model. *The Chronicle of Higher Education.*

Croissant, J. L. (2001, Sept-Oct). Can This Campus Be Bought? Commercial Influence in Unfamiliar Places. *Academe, 87,* 44–48.

Damrosch, D. (1995). *We Scholars: Changing the Culture of the University.* Cambridge, MA: Harvard University Press.

Datta, A. (2001, February 5). University Defends Its Spending on Fathom. *Columbia Spectator.*

Davis, S. M. (1984). *Managing Corporate Culture.* Cambridge, Massachusetts: Ballinger Publishing Company.

Davis, S. M., & Botkin, J. (1994). *The Monster Under the Bed: How Business is Mastering the Opportunity of Knowledge for Profit.* New York: Simon & Schuster.

Deal, T. E., & Kennedy, A. A. (1982). *Corporate Cultures: The Rites and Rituals of Corporate Life.* Reading, MA: Addison-Wesley Publishing Company.

Demb, A., & Neubauer, F. R. (1992). *The Corporate Board: Confronting the Paradoxes.* New York: Oxford University Press.

Dill, D. D. (2000). The Management of Academic Culture: Notes on the Management of Meaning and Social Integration. In M. C. Brown (Ed.), *Organization and Governance in Higher Education* (5th ed., pp. 261–272). Boston: Pearson Custom Publishing.

DiMaggio, P. J., & Powell, W. W. (1991). The Iron Cage Revisited: Institutional Isomorphism and Collective Rationality in Organizational Fields. In P. J. Dimaggio & W. W. Powell (Eds.), *The New Institutionalism in Organizational Analysis* (pp. 63–82). Chicago: University of Chicago Press.

Downey, J. (2000). Balancing Corporation, Collegium, and Community. In M. C. Brown (Ed.), *ASHE Reader on Organization and Governance in Higher Education* (5th ed., pp. 305–312). Boston: Pearson Custom Publishing.

Drucker, P. (1989, July/August). What Can Business Learn from Nonprofits? *Harvard Business Review*, 88–93.

Duderstadt, J. J. (2000a). *Fire, Ready, Aim! University Decision-making During an Era of Rapid Change.* Paper presented at the The Glion Colloquium II, San Diego, CA.

Duderstadt, J. J. (2000b). *A University for the 21st Century.* Ann Arbor: University of Michigan Press.

DukeCE. (2000a). Duke Corporate Education Ownership. Retrieved December 12, 2000, from http://www.dukece.com/company/company.html

DukeCE. (2000b). Our History. Retrieved December 12, 2000, from http://www.dukece.com/company/about.html

DukeCE. (2000c). People—Blair H. Sheppard. Retrieved December 8, 2000, from http://www.dukece.com/People/Sheppard.html

DukeCE. (2003). Duke Corporate Education: About Us. Retrieved February 4, 2003, from http://www.dukece.com/about_us/

Economist. (2001, February 17). Science and Profit. *The Economist*, 21.

Eklund, B. (2001, January 26). Street Talk: Wall Street Examines e-Learning. Retrieved 2001, January 30, from http://www.redherring.com/investor/2001/0126/inv-streettalk012601.html

Etzioni, A. (1964). *Modern Organizations.* Englewood Cliffs, NJ: Prentice-Hall.

Etzioni, A. (1975). *A Comparative Analysis of Complex Organizations: On Power, Involvement, and Their Correlates.* (Revised ed.). New York: Free Press.

Etzioni, A. (1991). Administrative and Professional Authority. In M. W. Peterson (Ed.), *Organization and Governance in Higher Education: An ASHE Reader* (4th ed., pp. 441–448). Needham Heights: Ginn Press.

Etzkowitz, H., Webster, A., & Healey, P. (Eds.). (1998). *Capitalizing Knowledge: New Intersections of Industry and Academia.* Albany, NY: State University of New York Press.

Evans, T., & Previte, L. (2001). NYUonline Thinks Small to Get Big. Retrieved January 23, 2001, from http://www.eduventures.com

Facets. (2001). *Facts About Columbia Essential To Students.* New York: Office of the Vice President for Student Services, Columbia University.

Fairweather, J. S. (1988). *Entrepreneurship and Higher Education.* Washington, D.C.: Association for the Study of Higher Education.

Farrell, E. F. (2002, July 19). U. of Oregon Offers Discount on Late-Afternoon Classes. *The Chronicle of Higher Education*, p. A33.

Fathom. (2000). About Fathom; Fathom Senior Team. Retrieved September 24, 2001, from http://www.fathom.com/about_revised/about_team.jhtml

Frye, B. (2001, October). Racing to Market. *University Business*, 4, 24.

Gates, G. S. (1997). Isomorphism, Homogeneity, and Rationalism in University Retrenchment. *Review of Higher Education, 20*(3), 253–275.

Gerber, L. G. (1997, September-October). Behind Closed Doors: Reaffirming the Value of Shared Governance. *Academe, 83*, 14–18.

Gerber, L. G. (2001, May-June). "Inextricably Linked": Shared Governance and Academic Freedom. *Academe, 87,* 22–24.

Gilbert, C. G. (2001). *A Dilemma in Response: Examining the Newspaper Industry's Response to the Internet.* Unpublished Dissertation, Harvard University Graduate School of Business Administration, Boston, Massachusetts.

Gilbert, C. G., & Bower, J. L. (2002, May). Disruptive Change: When Trying Harder is Part of the Problem. *Harvard Business Review,* 94–101.

Giroux, H. A. (1999). *Corporate Culture and the Attack on Higher Education and Public Schooling.* Bloomington, IN: Phi Delta Kappa Educational Foundation.

Giroux, H. A. (2001). Critical Education or Training: Beyond the Commodification of Higher Education. In H. A. Giroux & K. Myrsiades (Eds.), *Beyond the Corporate University: Culture and Pedagogy in the New Millennium* (pp. 1–12). Lanham, MD: Rowman & Littlefield Publishers, Inc.

Giroux, H. A., & Myrsiades, K. (Eds.). (2001). *Beyond the Corporate University: Culture and Pedagogy in the New Millennium.* Lanham, MD: Rowman & Littlefield Publishers.

Glick, W. H., Huber, G. P., Miller, C. C., Doty, D. H., & Sutcliff, K. M. (1995). Studying Changes in Organizational Design and Effectiveness. In G. P. Huber & A. H. Van de Ven (Eds.), *Longitudinal Field Research Methods* (pp. 126–154). Thousand Oaks, CA: Sage Publishing.

Glotzbach, P. A. (2001, May-June). Conditions of Collaboration: A Dean's List of Dos and Don'ts. *Academe, 87.*

Goldman, J. (2000, April 3). Venture Aims to Offer Reliable Citations on Web; Six Academic, Cultural Institutions Will Bring Expertise and New Information to Fathom Site, to Begin Later this Year. *The Los Angeles Times,* p. C1.

Goldstein, M. (1998, July). Alternative Strategies and Creating New Profit Possibilities. *Career Education Review,* 445–453.

Goldstein, M. (2000a). Financing Postbaccalaureate Education in an Age of Telecommunicated Learning. In K. J. Kohl & J. B. LaPidus (Eds.), *Postbaccalaureate Futures: New Markets, Resources, Credentials* (pp. 82–101). Phoenix, AZ: Oryx Press.

Goldstein, M. (2000b, September/October). To Be [For-profit] or Not To Be: What is the Question? *Change, 33,* 25–31.

Grimes, A. (2001, March 12). The Hope . . . and the Reality. *The Wall Street Journal.*

Gross, E., & Grambusch, P. V. (1968). *University Goals and Academic Power.* Washington, D.C.: American Council on Education.

Guba, E. G. (1978). *Toward a Methodology of Naturalistic Inquiry in Educational Evaluation.* Los Angeles: Center for the Study of Evaluation, UCLA Graduate School of Education.

Guba, E. G., & Lincoln, Y. S. (1981). *Effective Evaluation.* San Francisco: Jossey-Bass Publishers.

Gumport, P. J. (2000). Academic Restructuring: Organizational Change and Institutional Imperatives. *Higher Education, 39,* 67–91.

Gumport, P. J. (2001, Spring). Divided We Govern? *AAC&U Peer Review, 3,* 14–17.

Guterman, L. (2002, June 13). Medical Journal Eases Its Policy on Authors' Potential Conflicts of Interest. *The Chronicle of Higher Education.*

Guterman, L., & Werf, M. V. D. (2001, October 5). 12 Journals Adopt Joint Policy on Research Supported by Business. *The Chronicle of Higher Education*, p. A29.

Hafner, K. (2002, May 2). Lessons Learned at Dot-Com U. *The New York Times*, pp. E1, E8.

Hamilton, N. (2001, Spring). The Search for Common Ground on Academic Governance. *AAC&U Peer Review, 3,* 12–13.

Handbook. (2001, May 10). History and Traditions of New York University. In *New York University Faculty Handbook*. New York: New York University.

Hanley, L. (2002, July-August). Reappraising the Value of Shared Governance. *Academe, 88,* 2.

Hanley, L. (2002, September-October). Who Owns Your Ideas? *Academe, 88, 2.*

Harrison, M. I. (1994). *Diagnosing Organizations: Methods, Models, and Processes* (Second ed. Vol. 8). Thousand Oaks, CA: Sage Publications.

Hartley, J. F. (1994). Case Studies in Organizational Research. In C. Cassell & G. Symon (Eds.), *Qualitative Methods in Organizational Research: A Practical Guide* (pp. chapter 12). London: Sage.

Hollinger, D. A. (2001, May-June). Faculty Governance, The University of California, and the Future of Academe. *Academe, 87.*

Hult, K. M., & Walcott, C. (1990). *Governing Public Organizations: Politics, Structures, and Institutional Design*. Pacific Grove, CA: Brooks/Cole Publishing.

Ikenberry, S. O. (2001, Spring). The Practical and the Ideal: Striking a Balance. *The Presidency, 4,* 15–19.

Internal Revenue Code, 368 (2002).

Julius, D. J., Baldridge, J. V., & Pfeffer, J. (1999, March/April). A Memo from Machiavelli. *The Journal of Higher Education, 70*(2), 113–133.

June, A. W. (2002, August 16). Checking In on Campus. *The Chronicle of Higher Education*, p. A29.

Kanter, R. M. (1983). *The Change Masters: Innovation & Entrepreneurship in the American Corporation*. New York: Simon & Schuster, Inc.

Katz, S. N. (2001, June 15). In Information Technology, Don't Mistake a Tool for a Goal. *The Chronicle of Higher Education*, p. B7.

Keegan, P. (2000, December). The Web is Transforming the University. *Business 2.0.*

Kelly, K. F. (2001, July). *Meeting Needs and Making Profits: The Story of For-Profit Degree-Granting Institutions:* Education Commission of the States.

Kennedy, D. (1994). Making Choices in the Research University. In J. R. Coles, E. G. Barber & S. R. Graubard (Eds.), *The Research University in a Time of Discontent* (pp. 85–114). Baltimore, MD: Johns Hopkins University Press.

Kerr, C. (1994, January-February). Knowledge, Ethics, and the New Academic Culture. *Change,* 9–15.

Kezar, A. (2001). Seeking a Sense of Balance: Academic Governance in the 21st Century. *AAC&U Peer Review, 3,* 4–8.

Kezar, A., & Eckel, P. D. (2002). The Effect of Institutional Culture on Change Strategies in Higher Education. *The Journal of Higher Education, 73*(4), 435–460.

King, W. E. (2002). *Duke University: A Brief Narrative History.* Retrieved June 26, 2002, from www.duke.edu/web/Archives/history/narrativehistory.html

Klor de Alva, J. (2000, March/April). Remaking the Academy. *Educause Review,* 32–40.

Knight. (2001, March). *Policy Perspectives:* The Knight Higher Education Collaborative.

Kocijan, I. (1999, October 19). NYUonline, Inc. Announces Inaugural Certificate Program. Retrieved February 20, 2001, from http://www.nyu.edu/publicaffairs/newsreleases/b_NYUON.shtml

Kocijan, I. (2000, January 3). NYUonline, Inc. Names Gordon Macomber as New CEO. Retrieved February 20, 2001, from http://www.nyu.edu/publicaffairs/newsreleases/b_NYUON1.shtml

Kocijan, I. (2000, March 27). NYUonline, Inc. Builds Management Team. Retrieved February 20, 2001, from http://www.nyu.edu/publicarrairs/newsreleases/b_NYUON2.shtml

Konrad, R. (2001, March 6). E-learning Companies Look Smart Even in Down Market. Retrieved March 7, 2001, from http://news.cnet.com/news/0-1007-202-5043194.html

Kotter, J. P. (1996). *Leading Change.* Boston: Harvard Business School Press.

Kotter, J. P., & Heskett, J. L. (1992). *Corporate Culture and Performance.* New York: The Free Press.

Kuh, G. D., & Whitt, E. J. (1988). *The Invisible Tapestry: Culture in American Colleges and Universities* (ASHE-ERIC Higher Education Report No. 1). Washington, D.C.: ERIC Clearinghouse on Higher Education.

Kuh, G. D., & Whitt, E. J. (2000). Culture in American Colleges and Universities. In M. C. Brown (Ed.), *Organization and Governance in Higher Education* (5th ed., pp. 160–169). Boston, MA: Pearson Custom Publishing.

Kwartler, D. (2000, June). Babson & Duke Form Commercial Enterprises. *The MBA Newsletter,* pp. 1, 4, 6.

Leatherman, C. (1998, January 30). 'Shared Governance' Under Siege: Is It Time to Revive It or Get Rid of It? *The Chronicle of Higher Education,* p. A8.

Leibowitz, W. R. (2000, January 21). Law Professors Told to Expect Competition from Virtual Learning. *The Chronicle of Higher Education,* p. A45.

Leonard, M. (2002, September 3). On Campus, Comforts are Major. *Boston Globe,* p. A1.

Leonard-Barton, D. (1995). A Dual Methodology for Case Studies. In G. P. Huber & A. H. Van de Ven (Eds.), *Longitudinal Field Research Methods* (pp. 38–64). Thousand Oaks, CA: Sage Publications.

Letterman, D. (1999, October 20). *NYU to Offer Courses Online.* Retrieved February 20, 2001, from http://www.nyunews.com

Lindquist, B. (1999, February). Postsecondary Schools go For-Profit. *The Education Industry Report, 7,* 1–3, 11, 16.

Lorsch, J., & MacIver, E. (1989). *Pawns or Potentates: The Reality of America's Corporate Boards.* Boston: Harvard Business School Press.

Lowe, B. (2002, February 7). Fathoming Where the Money Goes. Retrieved February 19, 2002, from http://columbiaspectator.com/

Lynton, E. A. (1989, Sept-Oct). Higher Education in Partnership with Industry. *Journal of Higher Education, 60*(5), 612–614.

Maanen, J. V., Dabbs, J. M., & Faulkner, R. R. (1982). *Varieties of Qualitative Research.* Beverly Hills: Sage.

Mace, M. L. (1971). *Directors: Myth and Reality.* Boston: Harvard Business School.

Mahoney, R. J. (1997, October 7). 'Reinventing' the University: Object Lessons from Big Business. *The Chronicle of Higher Education,* p. B4.

Mallon, W. (2000). *Abolishing or Instituting Tenure: Four Case Studies of Change in Faculty Employment Policies.* Unpublished Dissertation, Harvard University, Cambridge, MA.

Mangan, K. S. (2000, November 1). Pharmaceutical Company Challenges Researchers' Finding That Drug Doesn't Counter HIV. *The Chronicle of Higher Education.*

Mangan, K. S. (2001, November 14). Duke's For-Profit Executive-Education Program Cuts Employees to Avoid a Deficit. *The Chronicle of Higher Education.*

March, J. G., & Olsen, J. P. (1976). *Ambiguity and Choice in Organizations.* Bergen, Norway: Universitetsforlaget.

Marshall, C., & Rossman, G. B. (1989). *Designing Qualitative Research.* Newbury Park, CA: Sage Publishing.

Martin, H. J. (1985). Managing Specialized Corporate Cultures. In R. H. Kilman, M. J. Saxton & R. Serpa (Eds.), *Gaining Control of the Corporate Culture* (pp. 148–162). San Francisco: Jossey-Bass Publishers.

Masland, A. (1991). Organizational Culture in the Study of Higher Education. In M. Peterson (Ed.), *Organization and Governance in Higher Education* (4th ed.). Needham Heights, MA: Simon & Schuster Custom Publishing.

Matrix. (2001, April). Matrix Unbound. Retrieved January 15, 2003, from http://www.universitybusiness.com/issues/story.asp?txtFilename=d:\webs\matrix\archives\apr01\frontier.html

Maxwell, J. A. (1996). *Qualitative Research Design: An Interactive Approach.* Thousand Oaks, CA: Sage Publications.

MBANewsletter. (2000, June). Babson & Duke Form Commercial Enterprises. *The MBA Newsletter,* pp. 1–6.

Merriam, S. B. (1988). *Case Study Research in Education: A Qualitative Approach.* San Francisco: Jossey-Bass Publishers.

Merritt, J. (2000, October 2). The Best B-Schools. *Business Week.*

Meyer, J. W., & Rowan, B. (1977). Institutionalized Organizations: Formal Structure as Myth and Ceremony. *American Journal of Sociology, 83*(2), 340–363.

Meyer, J. W., & Rowan, B. (1978). The Structure of Educational Organizations. In M. W. Meyer (Ed.), *Environments and Organizations: Theoretical and Empirical Perspectives* (pp. 79–109). San Francisco: Jossey-Bass Publishers.

Miles, M. B., & Huberman, A. M. (1994). *Qualitative Data Analysis* (2nd ed.). Thousand Oaks, CA: Sage Publications.

Millett, J. D. (1962). *The Academic Community.* New York: McGraw-Hill.

Minow, M. (2000, March 23). *Partners not Rivals?: Redrawing the Lines between Public and Private, Non-Profit and Profit, Secular and Religious.* Paper presented at the Boston University School of Law.

Monks, R. A. G., & Minow, N. (1995). *Corporate Governance*. Cambridge, MA: Blackwell Publishers Inc.

Mortimer, K. P., & McConnell, T. R. (1978). *Sharing Authority Effectively* (1st ed.). San Francisco: Jossey-Bass.

Myers, M. T. (2001, March 26). A Student is Not an Input. *The New York Times*, p. A23.

NACD. (2000). 1999–2000 Public Company Governance Survey. Retrieved 2001, March 23, 2001, March 23, from http://www.nacdonline.org/images/survey-sum.pdf

Nelson, C. (1997). *Manifesto of a Tenured Radical*. New York: New York University Press.

Nelson, C. (1999, April 16). The War Against the Faculty. *The Chronicle of Higher Education*, p. B4.

Newman, F. (2000, June 7). Are Faculty Members Losing Control as Colleges Create Online Divisions? Retrieved June 13, 2000, from http://chronicle.com/colloquylive/transcripts/2000/06/20000607newman.htm

Newman, F. (2002, April 26). *Competition and Market Forces: Higher Education Enters the Maelstrom of Transformation*. Providence, RI: The Futures Project: Policy for Higher Education in a Changing World.

Newman, F., & Couturier, L. (2001, June). *The New Competitive Arena: Market Forces Invade the Academy*. Providence, RI: The Futures Project: Policy for Higher Education in a Changing World.

Newman, F., & Couturier, L. (2001, October). University Competition Today: A More Unruly Market. *Current*, 12–17.

Noble, D. F. (1998). Digital Diploma Mills: The Automation of Higher Education. Retrieved July 6, 2000, from http://www.firstmonday.dk/issues/issue3_1/noble/index.html

NYU. (2000). New York University At a Glance. Retrieved November 7, 2000, from http://www.nyu.edu/introto.nyu

NYU. (2001). Historical Overview of the College. Retrieved March 1, 2001, from http://www.nyu.edu/cas/cashist.htm

NYUonline. (2001). Our Mission. Retrieved March 1, 2001, from http://www.nyuonline.com/vn_1/fpb/mission.html

NYUToday. (2000, October 26). New Book on NYU's History Illustrates 'The Miracle on Washington Square.' Retrieved April 10, 2001, from http://www.nyu.edu/nyutoday/archives/14/03/miracle.nyu

Oster, S. (1995). *Strategic Management for Nonprofit Organizations*. New York: Oxford University Press.

Ouchi, W. (1981). *Theory Z*. Reading, MA: Addison-Wesley.

Panus, M. (2000, June 30). Duke's Fuqua School of Business Forming Private Company. *Duke News Service Press Release*.

Patton, M. Q. (1990). *Qualitative Evaluation and Research Methods*. Newbury Park, CA: Sage Publications.

Peters, T. J., & Waterman, R. H. (1982). *In Search of Excellence: Lessons from America's Best-Run Companies*. New York: Warner Books.

Pfeffer, J., & Salancik, G. R. (1978). *External Control of Organizations: A Resource Dependence Perspective*. New York: Harper and Row.

Philpott, R. F. (1994). *Commercializing the University: The Costs and Benefits of the Entrepreneurial Exchange of Knowledge and Skills.* Unpublished Dissertation, University of Arizona, Tucson, AZ.

Posner, R. A. (2002, June). The University as Business. Retrieved June 10, 2002, from http://www.theatlantic.com/issues/2002/06/posner.htm

Pound, J. (2000). The Promise of the Governed Corporation. In H. B. Review (Ed.), *Harvard Business Review on Corporate Governance* (pp. 79–103). Boston: Harvard Business School Publishing.

Powers, D. R., Powers, M. F., Betz, F., & Aslanian, C. P. (1988). *Higher Education in Partnership with Industry.* San Francisco: Jossey-Bass.

Press, E., & Washburn, J. (2000, March). The Kept University. *The Atlantic Monthly, 39–53.*

Ramo, K. J. (1997). Reforming Shared Governance: Do the Arguments Hold Up? *Academe, 83,* 38–43.

Rewick, J. (2001, March 12). Off Campus. Retrieved March 19, 2001, from http://interactive.wsj.com/public/current/articles/SB984068778432368823.htm

Rhoden, W. C. (2002, July 25). Oregon Likes the Visibility of Broadway. *New York Times,* p. D1.

Rhodes, F. H. T. (2000, September). *The Glion Declaration II* (No. Occasional Paper No. 46): Association of Governing Boards of Colleges and Universities.

Rosenblatt, Z., Rogers, K. S., & Nord, W. R. (1993). Toward a Political Framework for Flexible Management of Decline. *Organization Science, 4,* 76–91.

Rosovsky, H. (1990). *The University: An Owner's Manual.* New York: W. W. Norton & Company.

Ruch, R. (1999, February). For Profit: Application of the Corporate Model to Academic Enterprise. *AAHE Bulletin, 51,* 3–6.

Ruch, R. (2001). *Higher Ed, Inc.* Baltimore: The Johns Hopkins University Press.

Rupp, G. (2000, February 29). Current Communications; President's Office. Retrieved September 21, 2001, from http://www.columbia.edu/cu/president/current.html

Ryan, W. (1999, January/February). The New Landscape for Nonprofits. *Harvard Business Review,* 127–136.

Sanford, T. (1984). Outrageous Ambitions. Retrieved December 20, 2002, from www.duke.edu/web/Archives/history/outrageous.html

Sansalone, M. (2000). Personal communication with author.

Schein, E. H. (1988). *Process Consultation: Its Role in Organization Development* (Vol. 1). Reading, MA: Addison-Wesley.

Schein, E. H. (1992). *Organizational Culture and Leadership* (2nd ed.). San Francisco: Jossey-Bass Publishers.

Schein, E. H. (1999). *The Corporate Culture Survival Guide.* San Francisco: Jossey-Bass.

Schmidt, P. (2002, March 29). States Push Public Universities to Commercialize Research. *The Chronicle of Higher Education,* pp. A26-A27.

Scott, J. W. (2002, July-August). The Critical State of Shared Governance. *Academe, 88,* 41–48.

Seidman, I. (1998). *Interviewing as Qualitative Research: A Guide for Researchers in Education and the Social Sciences* (2nd ed.). New York: Teachers College Press.

Senate. (2001). Resolution to Establish an Ad Hoc Committee on Online Learning and Digital Media Initiatives. Retrieved April 16, 2002, from http://www.columbia.edu/cu/senate/resolutions/00–01/onlinelearning.htm

Shea, C. (2001, September 16). Taking Classes to the Masses. *The Washington Post*, p. W25.

Sifonis, J. G., & Goldberg, B. (1996). *Corporation on a Tightrope: Balancing Leadership, Governance, and Technology in an Age of Complexity*. New York: Oxford University Press.

Silk, T. (1994). The Legal Framework of the Nonprofit Sector in the United States. In R. D. Herman (Ed.), *The Jossey-Bass Handbook of Nonprofit Leadership and Management* (pp. 65–82). San Francisco: Jossey-Bass.

Simon, J. G. (1987). The Tax Treatment of Nonprofit Organizations: A Review of Federal and State Policies. In W. W. Powell (Ed.), *The Nonprofit Sector: A Research Handbook* (pp. 67–98). New Haven, CT: Yale University Press.

Simpson, E. G. (2001). University Dot.Com: Are We Selling Out? *Continuing Higher Education Review, 65*, 49–59.

Slaughter, S. (2001, Sept-Oct). Professional Values and the Allure of the Market. *Academe, 87*, 22–26.

Slaughter, S., & Leslie, L. L. (1997). *Academic Capitalism: Politics, Policies, and the Entrepreneurial University*. Baltimore, MD: The Johns Hopkins University Press.

Smith, C. W. (2000). *Market Values in American Higher Education: The Pitfalls and Promises*. Lanham, MD: Rowman & Littlefield Publishers, Inc.

Soley, L. C. (1995). *The Corporate Takeover of Academia*. Boston: South End Press.

Sowell, T. (1998, September 7). An Outbreak of Sanity. *Forbes, 57*.

Stankiewicz, R. (1986). *Academics and Entrepreneurs: Developing University-Industry Relations*. New York: St. Martin's Press.

Steiner, D. (2000, August 7). Letter to the Editor. *The New York Times*, p. A22.

Stiles, P., & Taylor, B. (2001). *Boards At Work: How Directors View Their Roles and Responsibilities*. New York: Oxford University Press.

Suggs, W. (2000, January 14). Novel Corporate Deal Will Finance New Basketball Arena for U. of Maryland. *The Chronicle of Higher Education*, p. A54.

Tedeschi, B. (2001, March 12). E-Commerce: Pushing Ahead with Online Education. Retrieved March 12, 2001, from http://www.nytimes.com

Thompson. (2003). Subsidiaries of Tax-Exempt Organizations. Retrieved January 9, 2003, from www.t-tlaw.com/bus-04.shtml

Thompson, J. D. (1967). *Organizations in Action*. New York: McGraw-Hill.

Tierney, W. G. (1991). Organizational Culture in Higher Education: Defining the Essentials. In M. Peterson (Ed.), *Organization and Governance in Higher Education* (4th ed., pp. 126–139). Needham Heights, MA: Simon & Schuster Custom Publishing.

Tierney, W. G. (1999). *Building the Responsive Campus*. Thousand Oaks, CA: Sage Publications.

Til, J. V. (2000). When the Business of Nonprofits is Increasingly Business (Chapter 8). In *Growing Civil Society*. Bloomington, Indiana: Indiana University Press.

Totty, M., & Grimes, A. (2001, March 12). The Old College Try. *The Wall Street Journal*.

Tushman, M. L., Anderson, P., & O'Reilly, C. A. (1997). Technology Cycles, Innovation Streams, and Ambidextrous Organizations: Organization Renewal Through Innovation Streams and Strategic Change. In M. L. Tushman & P. Anderson (Eds.), *Managing Strategic Innovation and Change*. New York: Oxford University Press.

Tushman, M. L., & O'Reilly, C. A. (1996). Ambidextrous Organizations: Managing Evolutionary and Revolutionary Change. *California Management Review, 38*(4), 8–30.

Tushman, M. L., & O'Reilly, C. A. (1999). Building Ambidextrous Organizations: Forming Your Own "Skunk Works." *Health Forum Journal, 42*(2), 20–23.

USNews. (2003). *America's Best Colleges:* U.S. News & World Report.

Van Der Werf, M. (1999, October 15). As Coke and Pepsi Do Battle on Campuses, Colleges Find a Fountain of New Revenue. *The Chronicle of Higher Education*, p. A41.

Van Der Werf, M. (2001, September 13). University Prevails in Dispute with Pharmaceutical Company over HIV Drug. *The Chronicle of Higher Education*.

Van Der Werf, M., & Blumenstyk, G. (2001, March 2). A Fertile Place to Breed Businesses. *The Chronicle of Higher Education*, pp. A28-A30.

Weick, K. E. (1976). Educational Organizations as Loosely Coupled Systems. *Administrative Science Quarterly, 21*, 1–19.

Weick, K. E. (1982). Management of Organizational Change Among Loosely Coupled Elements. In P. S. Goodman & Associates (Eds.), *Change in Organizations* (pp. 375–408). San Francisco: Jossey-Bass.

Weick, K. E., & Orton, J. D. (1990). Loosely Coupled Systems: A Reconceptualization. *Academy of Management Review, 15*(2), 203–223.

Weisbrod, B. A. (1988). *The Nonprofit Economy.* Cambridge, MA: Harvard University Press.

Weisbrod, B. A. (1997). The Future of the Nonprofit Sector: Its Entwining with Private Enterprise and Government. *Journal of Policy Analysis and Management, 16*, 541–555.

Whitaker, R. (2001). Repositioning and Restructuring Continuing Education within the University. *Continuing Higher Education Review, 65*, 38–48.

Willis, E. (2001, May 28). Why Professors Turn to Organized Labor. *The New York Times*, p. A15.

Wilms, W. W., & Zell, D. M. (2002). *Awakening the Academy: A Time for New Leadership.* Bolton, MA: Anker Publishing Company.

Wilson, J. M. (2003, March). Is There a Future for Online Ed? *University Business, 6*, 7.

Winston, G. C. (1996, November). The Economic Structure of Higher Education: Subsidies, Customer-Inputs, and Hierarchy. Retrieved January 15, 2003, from http://www.williams.edu/wpehe

Winston, G. C. (1997, September/October). Why Can't a College Be More Like a Firm. *Change*, 32–38.

Winston, G. C., & Yen, I. C. (1995, July). Costs, Prices, Subsidies, and Aid in U.S. Higher Education. Retrieved January 15, 2003, from http://www.williams.edu/wpehe

Winston, G. C., & Zimmerman, D. J. (2000, May-June). Where Is Aggressive Price Competition Taking Higher Education? *Change*, 10–18.

Wojnarowski, A. (2002, August 9). Best of Times, Worst of Oregon's Times Square Billboard. Retrieved August 9, 2002, from http://espn.go.com

Wood, L. (2000, September 6). Out of Sight Need Not Mean Out of Mind. *Financial Times*, 2.

Yin, R. K. (1994). *Case Study Research: Design and Methods* (2nd ed.). Thousand Oaks, CA: Sage Publications.

Young, R. B. (1997). *No Neutral Ground: Standing by the Values We Prize in Higher Education*. San Francisco: Jossey-Bass Publishers.

Zusman, A. (1999). Issues Facing Higher Education. In P. Altbach, R. Berdahl & P. Gumport (Eds.), *American Higher Education in the Twenty-first Century* (pp. 107–148). Baltimore: The Johns Hopkins University Press.

Index

For Product Safety Concerns and Information please contact our EU
representative GPSR@taylorandfrancis.com Taylor & Francis Verlag GmbH,
Kaufingerstraße 24, 80331 München, Germany

Printed and bound by CPI Group (UK) Ltd, Croydon, CR0 4YY
08/06/2025
01896999-0008